# BRITISH RAILWAY DM

in Colour

## For the Modeller and Historian

Gavin Morrison

Ian Allan
PUBLISHING

*Previous page:* The Gloucester Railway Carriage & Wagon Co built the 'Cross-country' sets (later to become known as Class 119) that were introduced in October 1958 and used on longer-distance services on the Western Region. There were 28 sets, of which 25 were three-car units, the centre car being a Trailer Buffet Second (TRBS). Here a three-car set, complete with white cab roof, is seen leaving The Hawthorns Halt (near Handsworth Junction) as the 1.53pm Lapworth–Wellington on 16 September 1961. The halt was used only on days when there was a football match at the nearby West Bromwich Albion ground. *Michael Mensing*

*Below:* In 2008 Hull Trains leased some Class 180 'Adelantes' to work alongside and ultimately replace its Class 222 'Meridians'. No 180 111 is pictured at Wellbeck Normanton on its way back to Crofton depot, near Wakefield, following a crew-training run on 2 May 2008. *Gavin Morrison*

First published 2010

ISBN 978 0 7110 3472 3

Published by Ian Allan Publishing

an imprint of Ian Allan Publishing Ltd, Hersham, Surrey, KT12 4RG
Printed in England by Ian Allan Printing Ltd, Hersham, Surrey, KT12 4RG

Code: 1011/C1

Distributed in the United States of America and Canada by BookMasters Distribution Services

Visit the Ian Allan Publishing website at www.ianallanpublishing.com

# INTRODUCTION

Some 56 years have now elapsed since BR's first diesel multiple-units, the 'Derby Lightweights', were introduced on services between Leeds Central and Bradford Exchange. Of course, the railcar, in steam- or petrol-powered form, had been around since the early 1920s, and the development of diesel units would no doubt have progressed more quickly had not World War 2 intervened, but in Britain it was in the mid-1950s that the concept of the DMU really came into its own, when the railway authorities came to view its operation as a means of making branch lines viable.

It is fair to say that, like the diesel locomotives ordered in the wake of the 1955 Modernisation Plan, far too many types of DMU were built by too many manufacturers and without thorough testing, which resulted in many classes' giving plenty of trouble. As it became apparent to the BR Board that not even the DMUs could save many of the uneconomic services, so closures were made, resulting in a surplus of units, which fortunately allowed the less reliable classes to be withdrawn, and by the mid-1980s most of the Inter-City and many of the cross-country services that had had new DMUs built for them had reverted to locomotive haulage. Those classes that remained eventually had their problems solved, many continuing to give reasonable service to the end of the 1990s and beyond, and (with the exception of a handful of single cars, used for primarily for route-learning) the last examples of what were by now termed

A Class 142 'Pacer', in Arriva livery but without branding, is seen just east of Hexham on a working from Newcastle on 22 March 2006. *Gavin Morrison*

'heritage' units made their final journeys in December 2003, these being three Metro-Cammell units of Class 101 — arguably the most successful of the Modernisation Plan designs, comprising no fewer than 461 vehicles and spanning 47 years of service.

In the 1950s the Southern Region pursued a different path, opting for heavyweight construction and electric transmission that offered a high degree of standardisation with its existing fleet of electric units. The first of the Southern Region's diesel-electric multiple-units (DEMUs), introduced in 1957, were six-car units based on the BR Mk 1 carriage design but built to the restricted loading-gauge of the Hastings line, which resulted in a rather slab-sided appearance. They were followed later in the year by the first of a series standard-profile two- and three-car units for secondary and branch-line services in Hampshire, Berkshire and East Sussex. Somewhat dated even by the time of their introduction, they demonstrated noteworthy powers of longevity, the last examples (Classes 205 and 207) not being withdrawn until December 2004.

The DEMU concept was revived in the early 1980s, when, after an interval of nearly two decades, attention turned in earnest to replacement of the Modernisation Plan units. The result was Class 210, but after two prototype units had been built the decision was taken to concentrate on the simpler, diesel-hydraulic type, four prototype 'Sprinter' units — two each of the BREL (British Rail Engineering Ltd) Class 150 design and Metro-Cammell's rival Class 151 — appearing in 1983. Following extensive testing the Class 150, based on the Mk 3 coach body, was selected for further construction. As might be expected, these units were vastly superior in every respect

to the Modernisation Plan designs, and over the next 10 years numerous 'Sprinter'-type units were built by a variety of manufacturers, culminating in the Class 159 of 1992.

Also built during the 1980s were various types of 'Pacer' unit derived from the LEV prototype four-wheel railbus, which used a modified Leyland National bus bodyshell. Disliked by the public and enthusiasts alike, on account of their poor riding characteristics and sub-standard seating, these are now largely concentrated in the North of England and South Wales. However, it seems likely that, with the increase in patronage currently being enjoyed by the railways, they will be around for some years to come.

In 1997 came the first of the latest generation, in the form of the Class 168 'Clubman' units built by Adtranz (later Bombardier) in Derby; although the initial batch numbered just five units they were the forerunners of the Class 170 and 171 'Turbostars' that have subsequently entered service in substantial numbers in various parts of the country. Meanwhile Alstom in Birmingham was awarded contracts for construction of the Class 175 'Coradia' and high-speed Class 180 'Adelante' units, designed for longer-distance journeys, but although these were very pleasant trains in which to travel it must be said that in their early years they suffered their fair share of technical problems.

In 2000 came the first of the Bombardier-built Virgin 'Voyager', high-speed diesel-electric units, which found little favour with the public on account of their cramped interiors and paucity of luggage space, although their performance had generally been good, and the 'Pioneer' and 'Meridians' which followed had better internal layouts.

In 2005 Siemens Transportation of Germany broke into the market with the Class 185 'Desiro' sets for the Trans-Pennine services, which have performed well and liked by the public, although overcrowding is still a problem.

At the time of writing further 'Turbostar' units (Class 172) are awaited, but it seems likely that orders have now passed their peak and that henceforth most requirements will be met by cascading existing stock made redundant by the gradual spread of electrification.

This book seeks to portray the development of the DMU and DEMU from

1954 to the present day, and with this in mind I have chosen to use the pictures in chronological order, rather than deal with each class individually. This approach also emphasises the change in liveries from the sombre green and blue of BR days to the flamboyant schemes seen today. In a book of this size it would be impossible to illustrate every livery variation, but the vast majority have been included.

My thanks go to all those who have helped out with information and photographs. The humble Modernisation Plan DMUs were largely ignored by enthusiasts, most of whom occupied themselves with recording locomotive-hauled workings, but there were a few who photographed them in the early days, and without their contributions a book such as this would not have been possible. I am thus particularly grateful to Michael Mensing, as well to David Cross, for making available the collection of his later father, Derek.

If one's interests lie mainly in locomotives, opportunities for haulage or photography on the national rail network are nowadays extremely limited, but hopefully this book will demonstrate that, with its seemingly inexorable changes to rolling stock, franchises and liveries, the modern scene still has much to offer. It should also be borne in mind there are groups of dedicated enthusiasts who have restored many first-generation DMUs for operation on preserved lines, where, bedsides providing a useful back-up to more glamorous (but sometimes temperamental) locomotives, they offer a physical reminder of their contribution to Britain's railways over the past half-century.

*Gavin Morrison*
Mirfield
July 2010

## Bibliography
*abc Rail Guide* by Colin J. Marsden
   (Ian Allan, 2010)
*abc Traction Recognition* by
   Colin J. Marsden (Ian Allan, 2007)
*British Rail DMUs and Diesel Railcars*
   by Brian Morrison (Ian Allan, 1998)
*British Rail Fleet Survey 8: Diesel Multiple-
   Units — The First Generation* by Brian
   Haresnape (Ian Allan, 1985)
*British Rail Fleet Survey 9: Diesel Multiple-
   Units — The Second Generation and
   DEMUs* by Brian Haresnape
   (Ian Allan, 1986)
*British Railway First-Generation DMUs in
   Colour for the Modeller and Historian*
   by Stuart Mackay (Ian Allan, 2006)

*British Railway Pictorial: First-Generation
   DMUs* by Kevin Robertson
   (Ian Allan, 2004)
*The Heyday of the DMU*
   by Alan C. Butcher (Ian Allan, 1994)
*Motive Power Recognition 3: DMUs* by
   Colin J. Marsden (Ian Allan, 1982)
*The Second-Generation DMUs*
   by Colin J. Marsden (Ian Allan, 2008)

## Abbreviations
The following abbreviations were used by BR to identify types of vehicle used in DMU formations:

| | |
|---|---|
| DMBC | Driving Motor Brake Composite |
| DMBS | Driving Motor Brake Second |
| DMC | Driving Motor Composite |
| DMLV | Driving Motor Luggage Van |
| DMPV | Driving Motor Parcels Van |
| DMS | Driving Motor Second |
| DTC | Driving Trailer Composite |
| DTS | Driving Trailer Second |
| MBS | Motor Brake Second |
| MC | Motor Composite |
| MS | Motor Second |
| TBS | Trailer Brake Second |
| TC | Trailer Composite |
| TF | Trailer First |
| TRBF | Trailer Buffet First |
| TRBS | Trailer Buffet Second |
| TS | Trailer Second |

Addition of the letter 'L' in brackets — or 'K', in the case of corridor stock — signified the provision of lavatory facilities. Second was later classified as Standard.

## Coupling codes
Variations in types of transmission meant that not all units could work together. To distinguish units that could run together, the different control systems were coded as follows to ensure that only compatible vehicles were coupled together:

Red Triangle — Derby 'Lightweights' fitted with 125hp engine and torque converter; also Derby/Rolls-Royce four-car suburban Class 127

Yellow Diamond — Derby 'Lightweight' and Metropolitan-Cammell units fitted with 150hp engine and Wilson gearbox, and Cravens Class 129 parcels cars.

White Circle — Swindon Inter-City units for Scottish Region and Swindon Inter-City Class 126 units.

Orange Star — Derby three-car suburban Class 125 units.

Blue Square — All other standard transmission stock with AEC, Leyland or Rolls-Royce engines.

## Summary of second-generation DMUs and DEMUs

| Class | Number series | Type name |
|---|---|---|
| 140 | 140 001 | |
| 141 | 141 001-020 | |
| 142 | 142 001-096 | Pacer |
| 143 | 143 601-625 | Pacer |
| 144 | 144 001-023 | Pacer |
| 150/0 | 150 001/002 | Sprinter |
| 150/1 | 150 101-150 | Sprinter |
| 150/2 | 150 201-285 | Sprinter |
| 155 | 155 301-335 * | Super Sprinter |
| | 155 341-347 | Super Sprinter |
| 156 | 156 401-514 | Super Sprinter |
| 158/0 | 158 701-872 | Express |
| 158/9 | 158 901-910 | Express |
| 159/0 | 159 001-022 | |
| 165/0 | 165 001-039 | Networker Turbo |
| 165/1 | 165 101-137 | Networker Turbo |
| 166 | 166 201-221 | Network Express Turbo |
| 168/0 | 168 001-005 | Clubman |
| 168/1 | 168 106-113 | Clubman |
| 168/2 | 168 214-219 | Clubman |
| 170/1 | 170 101-117 | Turbostar |
| 170/2 | 170 201-208 | Turbostar |
| | 170 270-273 | Turbostar |
| 170/3 | 170 301-308 | Turbostar |
| | 170 392-399 | Turbostar |
| 170/4 | 170 401-434 | Turbostar |
| | 170 450-461 | |
| | 170 470-478 | |
| 170/5 | 170 501-523 | Turbostar |
| 170/6 | 170 630-639 | Turbostar |
| 171/7 | 171 721-729 | Turbostar |
| 171/8 | 171 801-806 | Turbostar |
| 172/0 | 172 001-008 | Turbostar |
| 172/1 | 172 101-104 | Turbostar |
| 172/2 | 172 211-222 | Turbostar |
| 172/3 | 172 331-345 | Turbostar |
| 175/0 | 175 001-011 | Coradia |
| 175/1 | 175 101-116 | Coradia |
| 180 | 180 101-114 | Adelante |
| 185 | 185 101-151 | Desiro |
| | | |
| 210 | 210 001/002 | |
| 220 | 220 001-034 | Voyager |
| 221 | 221 101-144 | Super Voyager |
| 222/1 | 222 101-104 | Pioneer |
| 222/4 | 222 008-023 | Meridian |
| 222/9 | 222 001-007 | Meridian |

* rebuilt 1991/2 by Andrew Barclay as single-car Class 153 units Nos 153 301-335/351-385

# First-generation diesel multiple-units and diesel-electric multiple-units

| No series | Built | Type | Class | Original Allocation | Notes |
|---|---|---|---|---|---|
| 50000-049 | Derby | DMBS | 114 | E | 2-car units |
| 50050-091 | Derby | DMBS | 116 | W | Suburban 3-car |
| 50092-133 | Derby | DMS | 116 | W | Suburban 3-car |
| 50134-137 | Met-Cam | DMBS | 111 | E | 2-car units |
| 50138-151 | Met-Cam | DMC | 101 | E | 4-car units |
| 50152-157 | Met-Cam | DMBS | 101 | E | 2-car units |
| 50158-163 | Met-Cam | DMC(L) | 101 | E | 2-car units |
| 50164-167 | Met-Cam | DMBS | 101 | E | 2-car units |
| 50168-171 | Met-Cam | DMC(L) | 101 | E | 2-car units |
| 50172-197 | Met-Cam | DMC | 101 | E | 4-car units |
| 50198-233 | Met-Cam | DMBS | 101 | M | 2-car units |
| 50234-245 | Met-Cam | DMC(L) | 101 | E | 4-car units |
| 50246-248 | Met-Cam | DMBS | 101 | E | 2-car units |
| 50249 | Cravens | DMBS | 105 | E | 4-car unit |
| 50250-259 | Met-Cam | DMBS | 101 | E | 2-car units |
| 50260-269 | Met-Cam | DMC(L) | 101 | E | 2-car units |
| 50270-279 | Met-Cam | DMC(L) | 111 | E | 3-car units |
| 50280-292 | Met-Cam | DMBS | 111 | E | 3-car units |
| 50293-296 | Met-Cam | DMBS | 101 | M | 2-car units |
| 50303-320 | Met-Cam | DMBS | 101 | M | 2-car units |
| 50321-338 | Met-Cam | DMC(L) | 101 | M | 3-car units |
| 50339-358 | Gloucester | DMBS | 100 | M/Sc | 2-car units |
| 50359-370 | Cravens | DMBS | 106 | E | 2-car units |
| 50371-394 | Cravens | DMBS | 105 | E | 2-car units |
| 50395-414 | Park Royal | DMBS | 103 | M | 2-car units |
| 50415-419 | Wickham | DMBS | 109 | E | 2-car units |
| 50420-423 | Birmingham | DMBS | 104 | M | 3-car units |
| 50424-427 | Birmingham | DMC(L) | 104 | M | 3-car units |
| 50428-479 | Birmingham | DMBS | 104 | M | 3-car units |
| 50480-531 | Birmingham | DMC(L) | 104 | M | 3-car units |
| 50532-541 | Birmingham | DMBS | 104 | M | 2-car units |
| 50542-593 | Birmingham | DMC(L) | 104 | E | 4-car units |
| 50594-598 | Birmingham | DMBS | 104 | E | 2-car units |
| 50599-629 | Derby | DMBS | 108 | E | 2 or 3-car units |
| 50630-646 | Derby | DMC(L) | 108 | E | 3 or 4-car units |
| 50647-695 | Swindon | DMS(L) | 120 | W | Cross-Country 3-car units |
| 50696-744 | Swindon | DMBC | 120 | W | Cross-Country 3-car units |
| 50745-751 | Met-Cam | DMC(L) | 101 | E | 3- or 4-car units |
| 50752-784 | Cravens | DMBS | 105 | M | 2- or 3-car units |
| 50785-817 | Cravens | DMC(L) | 105 | M | 2- or 3-car units |
| 50818-870 | Derby | DMBS | 116 | W | Suburban 3-car |
| 50871-923 | Derby | DMS | 116 | W | Suburban 3-car |
| 50924-935 | Derby | DMBS | 108 | M | 2-car units |
| 50936 | Swindon | DMS(L) | 126 | Sc | Inter-City 6-car units |
| 50938-987 | Derby | DMBS | 108 | M | 2-car units |
| 50988-1007 | Derby | DMS | 125 | E | Suburban 3-car |
| 51008-029 | Swindon | DMS(L) | 126 | Sc | Inter-City 6-car units |
| 51030-051 | Swindon | DMBS | 126 | Sc | Inter-City 3- or 6-car units |
| 51052-079 | Gloucester | DMBC | 119 | W | Cross-Country 3-car units |
| 51080-107 | Gloucester | DMS(L) | 119 | W | Cross-Country 3-car units |
| 51108-127 | Gloucester | DMBS | 100 | Sc | 2-car units |
| 51128-140 | Derby | DMBS | 116 | W | Suburban 3-car |
| 51141-153 | Derby | DMS | 116 | W | Suburban 3-car |
| 51154-173 | Derby | DMBS | 125 | E | Suburban 3-car |
| 51174-253 | Met-Cam | DMBS | 101 | M/E/Sc | 2-car units |
| 51254-301 | Cravens | DMBS | 105 | E | 2-car units |
| 51302-316 | Birmingham | DMBS | 118 | W | Suburban 3-car |
| 51317-331 | Birmingham | DMS | 118 | W | Suburban 3-car |
| 51332-373 | Pressed Steel | DMBS | 117 | W | Suburban 3-car |
| 51374-415 | Pressed Steel | DMS | 117 | W | Suburban 3-car |
| 51416-424 | Derby | DMBS | 108 | M | 2-car units |
| 51425-470 | Met-Cam | DMBS | 102 | E/Sc | 3- or 4-car units |
| 51471-494 | Cravens | DMBS | 105 | E/Sc | 2-car units |
| 51495-540 | Met-Cam | DMC(L) | 102 | E/Sc | 2-, 3- or 4-car units |
| 51541-550 | Met-Cam | DMBS | 111 | E | 2- or 3-car units |
| 51551-560 | Met-Cam | DMC(L) | 111 | E | 2- or 3-car units |
| 51561-572 | Derby | DMC(L) | 108 | M | 4-car Suburban |
| 51573-581 | Swindon | DMBC(L) | 120 | W | Cross-Country 3-car units |
| 51582-590 | Swindon | DMS(L) | 120 | W | Cross-Country 3-car units |
| 51591-650 | Derby | DMBS | 127 | M | Suburban 4-car |
| 51651-680 | Derby | DMBS | 115 | M | Suburban 4-car |
| 51681-705 | Cravens | DMBS | 112 | M | 2-car units |
| 51706-730 | Cravens | DMC(L) | 112 | M | 2-car units |
| 51731-755 | Cravens | DMBS | 113 | M | 2-car units |
| 51756-780 | Cravens | DMC(L) | 113 | M | 2-car units |
| 51781/2/7 | Swindon | DMBC | 120 | Sc | Cross-Country 3-car |
| 51783-786 | Swindon | DMBF | 120 | Sc | Cross-Country 3-car |
| 51788-794 | Swindon | DMS(L) | 120 | Sc | Cross-Country 3-car |
| 51795-801 | Met-Cam | DMBS | 102 | Sc | 3-car units |
| 51802-808 | Met-Cam | DMC(L) | 102 | Sc | 3-car units |
| 51809-828 | Birmingham | DMBC | 110 | E | 3-car units |
| 51829-848 | Birmingham | DMC(L) | 110 | E | 3-car units |
| 51849-900 | Derby | DMBS | 115 | M | Suburban 4-car |
| 51901-950 | Derby | DMBS | 108 | M | 2-car units |
| 51951-967 | Swindon | DMC | 124 | E | Trans-Pennine 6-car units |
| 51968-984 | Swindon | MBS(K) | 124 | E | Trans-Pennine 6-car units |
| 51985-2010 | Derby | DMBS | 107 | Sc | 3-car units |
| 52011-036 | Derby | DMC(L) | 107 | Sc | 3-car units |
| 52037-065 | Derby | DMC(L) | 108 | M | 2-car units |
| 52066-075 | Birmingham | DMBS | 110 | M | 3-car units |
| 52076-085 | Birmingham | DMC(L) | 110 | M | 3-car units |
| 52086-095 | Swindon | DMBS(L) | 123 | W | Inter-City 4-car |
| 52096-105 | Swindon | DMS(K) | 123 | W | Inter-City 4-car |
| 55000-019 | Gloucester | DMBS | 122 | W | Single cars |
| 55020-035 | Pressed Steel | DMBS | 121 | W | Single cars |
| 55987-996 | Gloucester | DMPV | 128 | M | Parcels vans |
| 55997-999 | Cravens | DMPV | 129 | M | Parcels vans |
| 56000-049 | Derby | DTC(L) | 114 | E | 2-car units |
| 56050-089 | Met-Cam | DTC(L) | 101 | E/M | 2-car units |
| 56090-093 | Met-Cam | DTC(L) | 111 | E/M | 2-car units |
| 56094-113 | Gloucester | DTC(L) | 100 | M/Sc | 2-car units |
| 56114-149 | Cravens | DTC(L) | 105 | E | 2-car units |
| 56150-169 | Park Royal | DTC(L) | 103 | M | 2-car units |
| 56170-174 | Wickham | DTC(L) | 109 | E | 2-car units |
| 56175-189 | Birmingham | DTC(L) | 104 | M/E | 2-car units |
| 56190-215 | Derby | DTC(L) | 108 | E/M | 2-car units |
| 56218-220 | Met-Cam | DTC(L) | 101 | NE | 2-car units |
| 56221-279 | Derby | DTC(L) | 108 | M | 2-car units |
| 56280-289 | Pressed Steel | DTS | 121 | W | 2-car units |
| 56291-299 | Gloucester | DTS | 122 | W | Single-unit trailers |
| 56300-319 | Gloucester | DTC(L) | 100 | Sc | 2-car units |
| 56332-411 | Met-Cam | DTC(L) | 101 | M/E/Sc | 2-car units |
| 56412-483 | Cravens | DTC(L) | 105 | E/Sc | 2-car units |
| 56484-504 | Derby | DTC(L) | 108 | M | 2-car units |
| 59000-031 | Derby | TC | 116 | M | Suburban 3-car |
| 59032-041 | Derby | TS | 116 | W | Suburban 3-car |
| 59042-048 | Met-Cam | TS(L) | 101 | E | 4-car units |
| 59049-055 | Met-Cam | TBS(L) | 101 | E | 4-car units |
| 59060-072 | Met-Cam | TS(L) | 101 | E | 4-car units |
| 59073-085 | Met-Cam | TBS(L) | 101 | E | 4-car units |
| 59086-091 | Met-Cam | TS(L) | 101 | E | 4-car units |
| 59092-097 | Met-Cam | TBS(L) | 101 | E | 4-car units |
| 59098-099 | Swindon | TRBF(K) | 126 | Sc | Inter City 3- or 6-car |
| 59100-109 | Met-Cam | TS(L) | 101 | E | 3-car units |
| 59112-113 | Met-Cam | TBS(L) | 101 | E | 4-car units |
| 59114-131 | Met-Cam | TC(L) | 101 | M | 3-car units |
| 59132-187 | Birmingham | TC(L) | 104 | M | 3-car units |
| 59188-208 | Birmingham | TS(L) | 104 | E | 4-car units |
| 59209-229 | Birmingham | TBS(L) | 104 | E | 4-car units |
| 59230-234 | Birmingham | TS(L) | 104 | E | 4-car units |
| 59235-239 | Swindon | TS(L) | 123 | W | Inter-City 4-car |
| 59240-244 | Birmingham | TBS(L) | 104 | E | 4-car units |

| No series | Built | Type | Class | Original Allocation | Notes |
|---|---|---|---|---|---|
| 59245-250 | Derby | TBS(L) | 108 | E | 4-car units |
| 59255-301 | Swindon | TRBS(L) | 120 | W | Cross-Country 3-car |
| 59302-306 | Met-Cam | TS(L) | 101 | E | 3- or 4-car units |
| 59307-325 | Cravens | TS(L)/TC(L) | 105 | M | 3-car units |
| 59326-376 | Derby | TC | 116 | W | Suburban 3-car |
| 59380-390 | Derby | TS(L) | 108 | E | 3- or 4-car units |
| 59391-400 | Swindon | TF(K) | 126 | Sc | Inter-City units |
| 59402-412 | Swindon | TC(L) | 126 | Sc | Inter-City units |
| 59413-437 | Gloucester | TRBS(L) | 119 | W | Cross-Country 3-car |
| 59438-448 | Derby | TC | 116 | W | Suburban 3-car |
| 59449-468 | Derby | TS | 125 | E | Suburban 3-car |
| 59469-483 | Birmingham | TC(L) | 118 | W | Suburban 3-car |
| 59484-522 | Pressed Steel | TC(L) | 117 | W | Suburban 3-car |
| 59523-568 | Met-Cam | TC(L) | 101 | E/Sc | 3- or 4-car units |
| 59569-572 | Met-Cam | TS(L) | 101 | E | 3-car units |
| 59573-578 | Met-Cam | TRBS(L) | 111 | E | 4-car units |
| 59579-588 | Swindon | TRBS(L) | 120 | W | Cross-Country 3-car |
| 59589-618 | Derby | TS(L) | 127 | M | Suburban 4-car |
| 59619-648 | Derby | TS | 127 | M | Suburban 4-car |
| 59649-663 | Derby | TS | 115 | M | Suburban 4-car |
| 59664-678 | Derby | TC(L) | 115 | M | Suburban 4-car |
| 59679-685 | Swindon | TRBS(L) | 120 | Sc | Cross-Country 3-car |
| 59686-692 | Met-Cam | TC(L) | 101 | Sc | 3-car units |
| 59693-712 | Birmingham | TS(L) | 110 | E | 3-car units |
| 59713-718 | Derby | TS | 115 | M | Suburban 4-car |
| 59719-724 | Derby | TC(L) | 115 | M | Suburban 4-car |
| 59725-744 | Derby | TS | 115 | M | Suburban 4-car |
| 59745-764 | Derby | TC(L) | 115 | M | Suburban 4-car |
| 59765-773 | Swindon | TS(L) | 124 | E | Trans-Pennine 6-car units |
| 59774-781 | Swindon | TRBF(L) | 124 | E | Trans-Pennine 6-car units |
| 59782-807 | Derby | TS(L) | 107 | Sc | 3-car units |
| 59808-817 | Birmingham | TS(L) | 110 | M | 3-car units |
| 59818-827 | Swindon | TC(K) | 123 | W | Inter-City 4-car units |
| 59828-832 | Swindon | TSRB(L) | 123 | W | Inter-City 4-car units |
| 79000-007 | Derby | DMBS | — | E | 2-car units |
| 79008-046 | Derby | DMBS | — | M/E | 2-car units |
| 79047-082 | Met-Cam | DMBS | — | E | 2-car units |
| 79083-111 | Swindon | DMBS(L) | 126 | W/Sc | Inter-City 6-car units |
| 79118-149 | Derby | DMBS | — | M/E | 2-car units |
| 79150-154 | Derby | DMS | — | E | 4-car units |
| 79155-168 | Swindon | DMS(L) | — | Sc | Inter-City 6-car units |
| 79169-181 | Derby | DMBS | — | M | 2-car units |
| 79184-188 | Derby | DMBS | — | M | 2-car units |
| 79189-190 | Derby | DMC(L) | — | M | 2-car units |
| 79191-193 | Derby | DTC(L) | — | M | Renumbered 79633-635 |
| 79250-262 | Derby | DTC(L) | — | M/E | 2-car units |
| 79263-291 | Met-Cam | DTS(L) | — | E | 2-car units |
| 79325-329 | Derby | TBS(L) | — | E | 4-car units |
| 79400-404 | Derby | TS(L) | — | E | 4-car units |
| 79440-447 | Swindon | TRBF(K) | 126 | W/Sc | Inter-City 6-car units |

| No series | Built | Type | Class | Original Allocation | Notes |
|---|---|---|---|---|---|
| 79470-482 | Swindon | TF(K) | 126 | W/Sc | Inter-City 6-car units |
| 79500-507 | Derby | DMC(L) | — | E | 2-car units |
| 79508-512 | Derby | DMC | — | E | 4-car units |
| 79600-625 | Derby | DTC(L) | — | M | 2-car units |
| 79626-632 | Met-Cam | DTC(L) | — | M | 2-car units |
| 79633-635 | Derby | DTC(L) | — | M | 2-car units |
| 79639-684 | Derby | DTC(L) | — | M | 2-car units |
| 79740 | ACV (BUT) | DMS | — | M | 3-car 4-wheel unit |
| 79741 | ACV (BUT) | TS | — | M | 3-car 4-wheel unit |
| 79742-744 | ACV (BUT) | DMBS | — | M | 3-car 4-wheel unit |
| 79745 | ACV (BUT) | DMS | — | M | 3-car 4-wheel unit |
| 79746-747 | ACV (BUT) | TS | — | M | 3-car 4-wheel unit |
| 79748 | ACV (BUT) | DMS | — | M | 3-car 4-wheel unit |
| 79749 | ACV (BUT) | TS | — | M | 3-car 4-wheel unit |
| 79750 | ACV (BUT) | DMBS | — | M | 3-car 4-wheel unit |
| 79900-901 | Derby | DMBS | — | M | Single units |
| 79958-959 | Bristol | Railbus | — | Sc | 4-wheel railbus |
| 79960-964 | W&M | Railbus | — | E | 4-wheel railbus |
| 79965-969 | Wickham | Railbus | — | Sc | 4-wheel railbus |
| 79970-974 | Park Royal | Railbus | — | Sc | 4-wheel railbus |
| 79975-979 | AC Cars | Railbus | — | Sc | 4-wheel railbus |

**Battery-electric railcars (included as based on DMU bodywork)**

| No series | Built | Type | Class | Original Allocation | Notes |
|---|---|---|---|---|---|
| 79998 | Derby/Cowlairs | DMBS | — | Sc | 2-car units |

**Diesel-electric multiple-units**

| No series | Built | Type | Class | Original Allocation | Notes |
|---|---|---|---|---|---|
| 60000-013 | Eastleigh | DMBS | 201 | S | Hastings units |
| 60014-031 | Eastleigh | DMBS | 202 | S | Hastings units |
| 60032-045 | Eastleigh | DMBS | 203 | S | Hastings units |
| 60090-093 | Met-Cam | DMBF(L) | 251 | M | Pullman 6-car units |
| 60094-099 | Met-Cam | DMBS | 251 | W | Pullman 8-car units |
| 60100-125 | Eastleigh | DMBS | 205 | S | Hampshire units |
| 60126-144 | Eastleigh | DMBS | 207 | S | Oxted units |
| 60145-151 | Eastleigh | DMBS | 205 | S | Hampshire units |
| 60500-520 | Eastleigh | TS(L) | 201 | S | Hastings units |
| 60521-547 | Eastleigh | TS(L) | 202 | S | Hastings units |
| 60548-561 | Eastleigh | TS(L) | 203 | S | Hastings units |
| 60600-618 | Eastleigh | TC(L) | 207 | S | Oxted units |
| 60644-649 | Met-Cam | DMBS(L) | 251 | W | Pullman 8-car units |
| 60650-678 | Eastleigh | TS | 205 | S | Hampshire units |
| 60700-706 | Eastleigh | TFK(L) | 201 | S | Hastings units |
| 60707-715 | Eastleigh | TFK(L) | 202 | S | Hastings units |
| 60716-722 | Eastleigh | TFK(L) | 203 | S | Hastings units |
| 60730-733 | Met-Cam | TKF(L) | 251 | M | Pullman 6-car units |
| 60734-739 | Met-Cam | TKF(L) | 251 | W | Pullman 8-car units |
| 60740-749 | Met-Cam | TPF(L) | 251 | M/W | Pullman 6 or 8-car units |
| 60750-756 | Eastleigh | TRB | 203 | S | Hastings units |
| 60800-832 | Eastleigh | DTC(L) | 205 | S | Hampshire units |
| 60900-918 | Eastleigh | DTS | 207 | S | Oxted units |

# Second-generation diesel multiple-units and diesel-electric multiple-units

| No series | Built | Type | Class | Notes |
|---|---|---|---|---|
| 50101-110 | Adtranz 1998/9 | DMS | 170/1 | 3-car units |
| 50111-117 | Adtranz 1998/9 | DMC | 170/1 | 2-car units |
| 50201-208 | Adtranz 1999 | DMC(L) | 170/2 | 3-car units |
| 50211-222 | Bombardier 2010 | DMS(L) | 172/2 | 2-car units |
| 50270-273 | Bombardier 2002 | DMS(L) | 170/2 | 3-car units |
| 50301-308 | Adtranz/Bombardier 2000/1 | DMC(L) | 170/3 | 2-car units |
| 50331-345 | Bombardier 2010 | DMS(L) | 172/3 | 3-car units |
| 50392 | Bombardier 2003 | DMC(L) | 170/3 | 2-car unit |
| 50393-398 | Bombardier 2003 | DMC(L) | 170/3 | 3-car units |
| 50399 | Adtranz 2000 | DMC(L) | 170/3 | 2-car unit |
| 50401-434 | Adtranz/Bombardier 1999-2005 | DMC(L) | 170/4 | 4-car units |
| 50450-461 | Adtranz/Bombardier 1999-2005 | DMS(L) | 170/4 | 4-car units |

| No series | Built | Type | Class | Notes |
|---|---|---|---|---|
| 50470-478 | Adtranz/Bombardier 1999-2005 | DMS(L) | 170/4 | 4-car units |
| 50501-523 | Adtranz 1999-2000 | DMS(L) | 170/5 | 2-car units |
| 50630-639 | Adtranz 1999-2000 | DMS(L) | 170/6 | 3-car units |
| 50701-711 | Alstom 1999-2001 | DMS(L) | 175/0 | 2-car units |
| 50721-729 | Bombardier 2003 | DMC(L) | 171/7 | 2-car units |
| 50751-766 | Alstom 1999-2001 | DMS(L) | 175/1 | 3-car units |
| 50801-806 | Bombardier 2003 | DMC(L) | 171/8 | 4-car units |
| 50901-914 | Alstom 2000-2 | DMS(L) | 180 | 5-car units |
| 51101-151 | Siemens 2005/6 | DMC(L) | 185 | 3-car units |
| 52101-150 | BREL York 1985/6 | DMS(L) | 150/1 | 2-car units |
| 52201-285 | BREL York 1986/7 | DMS(L) | 150/2 | 2-car units |
| 52301-335 | Leyland 1987/8 | DMS(L) | 155 | 2-car units |

| No series | Built | Type | Class | Notes |
|-----------|-------|------|-------|-------|
| 52314-347 | Leyland 1988 | DMS(L) | 155 | 2-car units |
| 52401-514 | Metro-Cammell 1987-9 | DMS(L) | 156 | 2-car units |
| 52701-872 | BREL Derby 1989-92 | DMS(L) | 158/0 | 2-car units |
| 52873-98894 | BREL Derby 1992 | DMC(L) | 159 | 3-car units |
| 52901-910 | BREL Derby 1991 | DMS(L) | 158/9 | 2-car units |
| 53101-151 | Siemens 2005/6 | MS(L) | 185 | 3-car units |
| 54101-151 | Siemens 2005/6 | DMC(L) | 185 | 3-car units |
| 54801-806 | Bombardier 2003 | MS | 171/8 | 4-car units |
| 54901-914 | Alstom 2000-2 | MF(L) | 180 | 5-car units |
| 55101-110 | Adtranz 1998/9 | MC | 170/1 | 3-car units |
| 55200-201 | BREL York 1984 | DMS(L) | 150 | 3-car units |
| 55202-203 | Metro-Cammell 1985 | DMS(L) | 151 | 3-car units |
| 55300-301 | BREL York 1984 | DMS | 150 | 3-car units |
| 55302-303 | Metro-Cammell 1985 | DMS | 151 | 3-car units |
| 55400-401 | BREL York 1984 | MS | 150 | 3-car units |
| 55402-403 | Metro-Cammell 1985 | MS | 151 | 3-car units |
| 55404-414 | BREL/ABB York 1990-2 | MS | 165/0 | 3-car units |
| 55415-431 | BREL/ABB York 1990-2 | MS | 165/1 | 3-car units |
| 55500 | BREL Derby / Leyland 1981 | DMS | 140 | 2-car unit |
| 55501 | BREL Derby / Leyland 1981 | DMS(L) | 140 | 2-car unit |
| 55502-521 | BREL Derby / Leyland 1983 | DMS | 141 | 2-car units |
| 55522-541 | BREL Derby / Leyland 1983 | DMS(L) | 141 | 2-car units |
| 55542-591 | BREL Derby / Leyland 1985-7 | DMS | 142 | 4-car units |
| 55592-641 | BREL Derby / Leyland 1985-7 | DMS(L) | 142 | 4-car units |
| 55642-666 | A. Barclay / Alexander 1985/6 | DMS | 143 | 2-car units |
| 55667-691 | A. Barclay / Alexander 1985/6 | DMS(L) | 143 | 2-car units |
| 55701-746 | BREL Derby / Leyland 1985-7 | DMS | 142 | 4-car units |
| 55747-792 | BREL Derby / Leyland 1985-7 | DMS(L) | 142 | 4-car units |
| 55801-823 | BREL Derby / Alexander 1986/7 | DMS | 144 | 2-car units |
| 55850-859 | BREL Derby / Alexander 1986/7 | MS | 144 | 3-car units |
| 55824-846 | BREL Derby / Alexander 1986/7 | DMS(L) | 144 | 2-car units |
| 55901-914 | Alstom 2000-2 | MS(L) | 180 | 5-car units |
| 56201-208 | Adtranz 1999 | MS(L) | 170/2 | 3-car units |
| 56331-345 | Bombardier 2010 | MS | 172/3 | 3-car units |
| 56393-398 | Bombardier 2003 | MS(L)RB | 170/3 | 3-car units |
| 56630-639 | Adtranz 1999-2000 | MS | 170/6 | 3-car units |
| 56401-434 | Adtranz/Bombardier 1999-2005 | MS(L) | 170/4 | 4-car units |
| 56450-461 | Adtranz/Bombardier 1999-2005 | MS(L) | 170/4 | 4-car units |
| 56470-478 | Adtranz/Bombardier 1999-2005 | MS(L) | 170/4 | 4-car units |
| 56751-766 | Alstom 1999-2001 | MS(L) | 175/1 | 3-car units |
| 56801-806 | Bombardier 2003 | MS | 171/8 | 4-car units |
| 56901-914 | Alstom 2000-2 | MS(L)RB | 180 | 5-car units |
| 57101-150 | BREL York 1985/6 | DMS | 150/1 | 2-car units |
| 57201-285 | BREL York 1986/7 | DMS | 150/2 | 2-car units |
| 57301-335 | Leyland 1987/8 | DMS(L) | 155 | 2-car units |
| 57341-347 | Leyland 1988 | DMS | 155 | 2-car units |
| 57401-514 | Metro-Cammell 1987-9 | DMS | 156 | 2-car units |
| 57701-872 | BREL Derby 1989-92 | DMS(L) | 158/0 | 2-car units |
| 57873-894 | BREL Derby 1992 | DMS(L) | 159 | 3-car units |
| 57901-910 | BREL Derby 1991 | DMS | 158/9 | 2-car units |
| 58101-121 | BREL/ABB York 1992/3 | DMC(L) | 166 | 3-car units |
| 58122-142 | BREL/ABB York 1992/3 | DMC(L) | 166 | 3-car units |
| 58151-155 | Adtranz 1997/8 | DMS(L) | 168/0 | 4-car units |
| 58156-163 | Adtranz/Bombardier 2000/2 | DMS(L) | 168/1 | 3- / 4-car units |
| 58164-169 | Bombardier 2003/4 | DMS(L) | 168/2 | 3- / 4-car units |
| 58251-255 | Adtranz 1997/8 | DMS(L) | 168/0 | 4-car units |
| 58256-263 | Adtranz/Bombardier 2000/2 | DMS(L) | 168/1 | 3- / 4-car units |
| 58264-269 | Bombardier 2003/4 | DMS(L) | 168/2 | 3- / 4-car units |
| 58365-367 | Bombardier 2006 | MS | 168/2 | 4-car units |
| 58451-455 | Adtranz 1997/8 | MS | 168/0 | 4-car units |
| 58456-463 | Adtranz/Bombardier 2000/2 | MS(L) | 168/1 | 3- / 4-car units |
| 58464-469 | Bombardier 2003/4 | MS | 168/2 | 3- / 4-car units |
| 58601-621 | BREL/ABB York 1992/3 | MS | 166 | 3-car units |
| 58651-655 | Adtranz 1997/8 | MS(L) | 168/0 | 4-car units |
| 58718-739 | BREL Derby 1992 | MS(L) | 159 | 3-car units |
| 58756-757 | Bombardier 2000 | MS | 168/1 | 4-car units |
| 58801-822 | BREL/ABB York 1990-2 | DMC(L) | 165/0 | 2-car units |
| 58823-833 | BREL/ABB York 1990-2 | DMC(L) | 165/0 | 3-car units |
| 58834-855 | BREL/ABB York 1990-2 | DMS | 165/0 | 2-car units |
| 58856-866 | BREL/ABB York 1990-2 | DMS | 165/0 | 3-car units |
| 58867-872 | BREL/ABB York 1990-2 | DMS | 165/0 | 2-car units |
| 58873-878 | BREL/ABB York 1990-2 | DMC(L) | 165/0 | 2-car units |
| 58916-932 | BREL/ABB York 1990-2 | DMC(L) | 165/1 | 3-car units |
| 58953-969 | BREL/ABB York 1990-2 | DMS | 165/1 | 3-car units |
| 58879-898 | BREL/ABB York 1990-2 | DMC(L) | 165/1 | 2-car units |
| 58933-952 | BREL/ABB York 1990-2 | DMS | 165/1 | 2-car units |
| 59111-114 | Bombardier 2010/1 | DMS | 172/1 | 2-car units |
| 59211-214 | Bombardier 2010/1 | DMS | 172/1 | 2-car units |
| 59311-318 | Bombardier 2010/1 | DMS | 172/0 | 2-car units |
| 59411-418 | Bombardier 2010/1 | DMS | 172/0 | 2-car units |
| 59901-914 | Alstom 2000-2 | DMS(L) | 180 | 5-car units |
| 79101-110 | Adtranz 1998/9 | DMS | 170/1 | 3-car units |
| 79111-117 | Adtranz 1998/9 | DMC | 170/1 | 3-car units |
| 79201-208 | Adtranz 1999 | DMS(L) | 170/2 | 3-car units |
| 79211-222 | Bombardier 2010 | DMS | 172/2 | 2-car units |
| 79270-273 | Bombardier 2002 | DMC(L) | 170/2 | 3-car units |
| 79301-308 | Adtranz/Bombardier 2000/1 | DMC(L) | 170/3 | 2-car units |
| 79331-345 | Bombardier 2010 | DMS | 172/3 | 3-car units |
| 79392 | Bombardier 2003 | DMC(L) | 170/3 | 2-car unit |
| 79393-398 | Bombardier 2002/3 | DMC(L) | 170/3 | 3-car units |
| 79399 | Adtranz 2000 | DMC(L) | 170/3 | 2-car units |
| 79401-434 | Adtranz/Bombardier 1999-2005 | DMC(L) | 170/4 | 4-car units |
| 79450-461 | Adtranz/Bombardier 1999-2005 | DMC(L) | 170/4 | 4-car units |
| 79470-478 | Adtranz/Bombardier 1999-2005 | DMC(L) | 170/4 | 4-car units |
| 79501-523 | Adtranz 1999-2000 | DMS(L) | 170/5 | 2-car units |
| 79630-639 | Adtranz 1999-2000 | DMS(L) | 170/6 | 3-car units |
| 79721-729 | Bombardier 2003 | DMS(L) | 171/7 | 2-car units |
| 79701-711 | Alstom 1999-2001 | DMS(L) | 175/0 | 2-car units |
| 79751-766 | Alstom 1999-2001 | DMS(L) | 175/1 | 3-car units |
| 79801-806 | Bombardier 2003 | DMS(L) | 171/8 | 4-car units |

### Diesel-electric multiple-units

| No series | Built | Type | Class | Notes |
|-----------|-------|------|-------|-------|
| 60161-167 | Bombardier 2004 | DMS(L) | 222/9 | 9-car units |
| 60168-183 | Bombardier 2004/5 | DMS(L) | 222/4 | 4-car units |
| 60191-194 | Bombardier 2005 | DMS(L) | 222/1 | 4-car units |
| 60200 | BREL Derby 1981 | DMS | 210 | 3-car unit |
| 60201 | BREL Derby 1981 | DMBS | 210 | 4-car unit |
| 60201-234 | Bombardier 2000/1 | MS(L) | 220 | 4-car units |
| 60241-247 | Bombardier 2004/5 | DMS(L) | 222/9 | 9-car units |
| 60248-263 | Bombardier 2004/5 | DMRF(L) | 222/4 | 4-car units |
| 60271-274 | Bombardier 2005 | DMS(L) | 222/1 | 4-car units |
| 60300 | BREL Derby 1981 | DTS | 210 | 4-car unit |
| 60301 | BREL Derby 1981 | DTS | 210 | 3-car unit |
| 60301-334 | Bombardier 2000/1 | DMS(L) | 220 | 4-car units |
| 60341-347 | Bombardier 2004/5 | MF(L) | 222/9 | 9-car units |
| 60351-390 | Bombardier 2002/3 | DMS(L) | 221 | 5-car units |
| 60391-394 | Bombardier 2002/3 | DMS(L) | 221 | 4-car units |
| 60400 | BREL Derby 1981 | TS | 210 | 3-car unit |
| 60401 | BREL Derby 1981 | TS | 210 | 4-car unit |
| 60401-434 | Bombardier 2002/3 | MF(L) | 220 | 4-car units |
| 60441-447 | Bombardier 2004/5 | MS(L) | 222/9 | 9-car units |
| 60450 | BREL Derby 1981 | TC(L) | 210 | 4-car unit |
| 60451-490 | Bombardier 2002/3 | DMF(L) | 221 | 5-car units |
| 60491-494 | Bombardier 2002/3 | DMF(L) | 221 | 4-car units |
| 60531-537 | Bombardier 2004/5 | MS(L) | 222/9 | 9-car units |
| 60541-547 | Bombardier 2004/5 | MS(L) | 222/9 | 9-car units |
| 60551-557 | Bombardier 2004/5 | MS(L) | 222/9 | 9-car units |
| 60561-567 | Bombardier 2004/5 | MS(L) | 222/9 | 9-car units |
| 60571-574 | Bombardier 2005 | MS(L) | 222/1 | 4-car units |
| 60621-627 | Bombardier 2004/5 | MSRMB | 222/9 | 9-car units |
| 60628-643 | Bombardier 2004/5 | MSRMB | 222/4 | 4-car units |
| 60681-684 | Bombardier 2005 | MSRMB | 222/1 | 4-car units |
| 60701-734 | Bombardier 2000/1 | MS(L) | 220 | 4-car units |
| 60751-790 | Bombardier 2002/3 | MS(L) | 221 | 5-car units |
| 60791-794 | Bombardier 2002/3 | MS(L) | 221 | 4-car units |
| 60851-890 | Bombardier 2002/3 | MS(L) | 221 | 5-car units |
| 60918-933 | Bombardier 2004/5 | MC(L) | 222/4 | 4-car units |
| 60951-990 | Bombardier 2002/3 | MS(L) | 221 | 5-car units |
| 60991-994 | Bombardier 2002/3 | MS(L) | 221 | 4-car units |

*Above:* The Gloucester 'Cross-Country' units (Class 119) were fitted with two AEC or Leyland six-cylinder 150hp engines. Most were formed as three-car sets, but three entered service as twins. Here an immaculate three-car set, with DMS(L) No W51099 leading, prepares to leave Acocks Green & South Yardley on 4 July 1959 as the 1.20pm Birmingham Moor Street–Leamington Spa General. *Michael Mensing*

*Below:* The first Modernisation Plan DMUs to appear were 49 two-car units (later Class 114) built by BR at Derby. Introduced in 1956, they were allocated to Eastern Region services, mainly in Lincolnshire; here a four-car formation, with DTC(L) No E56038 leading, departs Grantham for Lincoln on 5 September 1959. Included in the refurbishment programme of the 1970s, the Class 114s ultimately put in more than 30 years' service, the final example not being withdrawn until 1992. *Gavin Morrison*

In 1955 Park Royal Vehicles won an order to build 20 two-car units, which later became known collectively as Class 103. Each unit had a six-cylinder AEC engine of 150hp. They were introduced in 1957, mainly in the West Midlands; here DMBS No M50395 heads a four-car formation calling at Redditch in 1960. Bringing up the rear is a Metro-Cammell two-car unit (later Class 101). *Michael Mensing*

Ten Motor Luggage Vans were built by the Gloucester Railway Carriage & Wagon Co and introduced from January 1960. Powered two six-cylinder Leyland Albion 230hp engines, which provided sufficient power to haul extra vans, they were employed initially on the Western and London Midland Regions; later known as Class 128, they lasted in service until 1990. Here, on Sunday 30 July 1961, No W55998 and a bogie parcels van arrive at Prince's End & Coseley station, between Wolverhampton and Stourbridge Junction, on a service run for the benefit of pigeon-fanciers. *Michael Mensing*

By far the most glamorous of the early DMUs were the 'Blue Pullman' sets built in 1960 by Metro-Cammell of Birmingham. Two of these were six-car units for on prestige services on the Midland main line between London St Pancras and Manchester Central — primarily to provide executive travel for business customers during the electrification of the West Coast main line. The six-car sets accommodated 132 First-class passengers. Each powered by two 1,000hp MAN engines assembled by the North British Locomotive Co, the units had GEC main generators supplying DC power for traction and an auxiliary generator supplying battery-chargers, control circuits, compressors and cab heaters; two Rolls-Royce eight-cylinder diesel engines supplied AC power for lighting, air-conditioning etc. There were also three eight-car sets for Western Region services between Paddington and Bristol or Wolverhampton, one of which is pictured near Acocks Green on the 1.0pm Birmingham Snow Hill–Paddington on 12 October 1961, showing to good advantage the units' striking livery of Nanking blue and white. *Michael Mensing*

Built by Cravens and introduced in July 1958 were three Motor Luggage Vans (later Class 129), allocated initially to Newton Heath depot in Manchester. Equipped with two 150hp six-cylinder AEC engines, they were easily capable of towing extra vans. No M55998 is shown at Birmingham New Street's Platform 5 after arrival from the Coventry direction on 4 August 1962. They had relatively short careers, being withdrawn in 1972/3, although one (formerly No M55997) lasted until 1986, working for the Derby Research Centre as No RDB975385. *Michael Mensing*

*Above:* Introduced in 1957, the Swindon-built 'Inter-City' sets (TOPS Class 126) were intended primarily for services between Glasgow and Edinburgh as well as down the coast as far as Stranraer. With DMBS(L) No SC51045 leading, a six-car formation leaves Stranraer Harbour for Glasgow St Enoch at 1.30pm on 12 July 1963. Ultimately passenger numbers on the Glasgow–Edinburgh services outgrew the capacity of the six-car formations, which were replaced by hauled stock powered by BRCW Type 2 (Class 27) locomotives working in push-pull mode, and it is the Ayrshire services with which the '126s' will always be most readily associated. *Michael Mensing*

*Left:* On 14 May 1964 a Gloucester RCW diesel parcels car (later Class 128) passes Old Hill station, between Birmingham Snow Hill and Stourbridge Junction, on a down working. *Michael Mensing*

*Right:*February 1963 saw the introduction of Swindon-built three- and four-car 'Inter-City' units (TOPS Class 123) powered by four Leyland Albion six-cylinder engines of 230hp. The 10 sets operated initially on Swansea–Birmingham–Derby services; here, on 22 August 1964, DMBS(L) No W52091 is the leading vehicle of an eight-car formation descending the Lickey Incline as train 1V72, the 5.20pm Derby Midland–Cardiff General. *Michael Mensing*

*Below:*A Birmingham Railway Carriage & Wagon Co (Class 104) driving motor is the lead vehicle of a very mixed DMU formation seen at the unusual location of Pateley Bridge on 12 March 1964. This was quite possibly the only time a DMU visited this location, for passenger services had been withdrawn in April 1951, and the line was destined to close altogether in October 1964. The train was a special was run for the benefit of local schoolchildren, many of whom had never travelled by train, it being considered a good idea to give them the experience while the opportunity still existed. *Gavin Morrison*

The Southern Region adopted a different approach to diesel multiple-units, preferring electric transmission to the simpler mechanical system employed elsewhere. Here, on 11 September 1964 No 1103, one of its three-car Class 3H (later 205) 'Hampshire' DEMUs, in original green livery, leaves Southampton on a down working. There were four batches built, Nos 1101-18 of 1957 being followed by Nos 1119-22, for the Ashford–Hastings line; so successful were these that a further four sets (Nos 1123-6) were built in 1959, and finally another seven (Nos 1127-33) entered service in 1962 on Reading–Salisbury services. All were ultimately fitted with two English Electric engines of 600hp (the earlier units being uprated from 500hp), giving a total output per unit of 1,200hp. Withdrawal began in 1987, but 11 three-car units survived long enough to be used by Connex SouthCentral. *Gavin Morrison*

*Above:* To supplement deliveries from Swindon Works the Western Region turned in 1959 to the Birmingham Railway Carriage & Wagon Co (BRCW) for the supply of 15 high-density three-car units (later Class 118), one of which is pictured at Axminster station on an up working on 28 February 1965. To the left are two Ivatt 2-6-2T steam locomotives taking water in the bay platform awaiting the arrival of a special from Waterloo for a trip over the Lyme Regis branch. *Gavin Morrison*

*Right:* The first examples of the Swindon-built three-car 'Inter-City' units (later Class 126) were ordered for the Western and Scottish Regions and were introduced in 1956/7. Powered by four BUT (AEC) six-cylinder 150hp engines, they were unusual in that one end (only) of each unit was equipped with a corridor connection, allowing two three-car sets to be made up into a six-car formation with a corridor connection throughout. On 3 July 1965, however, a six-car formation, with 'intermediate' DMS(L) No SC51016 leading, is pictured arriving at Pinwherry (roughly halfway between Ayr and Stranraer), where the signalman will exchange tokens with the crew. *Derek Cross*

Introduced in 1954, the 'Derby Lightweights', as they became known, were the first DMUs to be built in quantity by British Railways. They comprised two single cars, 12 'power twin' two-car units, 84 power/trailer two-car units and four four-car units. Fitted with BUT (Leyland) engines developing 125hp, they were capable of a maximum speed of 62mph. Their introduction on services between Leeds Central and Bradford Exchange proved a great success, encouraging the BR Board to order many more units from various manufacturers. They eventually moved to the London Midland Region, taking over local services in Cumbria; this two-car set is seen near Penrith, heading for Keswick, on 17 July 1965. By the late 1960s the 'Derby Lightweights' were regarded as non-standard, and all were withdrawn by the end of the decade. *Michael Mensing*

Thirty three-car 'Calder Valley' (Class 110) sets were constructed by the Birmingham Railway Carriage & Wagon Co at Smethwick. They were similar to the earlier BRCW units (Class 104), they were identifiable by the four-character headcode displays above the cabs and were equipped with four Rolls-Royce six-cylinder engines of 180hp (*i.e.* two in each driving vehicle), giving a total output per unit of 720hp, the extra power being needed to tackle the 1-in-50 gradients encountered around Bradford on the Leeds–Manchester services. All were in service by January 1962, and they lasted until 1992, albeit from 1983 mainly as two-car sets. Here, on 17 July 1965, a six-car formation passes through Arthington station (closed in March of that year) as the 16.33 Harrogate–Leeds Central. *Michael Mensing*

The Metropolitan-Cammell units — later Classes 101 and 102 — were by far the most numerous of the BR DMUs. In all some 637 vehicles were built, of which 364 were powered. What became known as the Class 101s were fitted with two BUT (AEC) six-cylinder 150hp engines, the '102s' being Leyland-powered. They were introduced in 1956, the last entering service in 1960. They were configured as two-, three- and four-car sets; here we see a two-car set headed by DTC(L) No 56381, in BR green, ready to leave Morecambe Promenade on 9 October 1965. In due course they were to see service on all regions. Most units would receive a major refurbishment in the mid-1970s, and the last survivor would not be withdrawn until December 2003. *Gavin Morrison*

Having arrived at Birmingham Snow Hill on the up 'Western Pullman' (10.10 ex Paddington) on 11 October 1966, one of the eight-car 'Blue Pullman' sets crosses to the up platform ready to depart on the 13.00 return working. Following electrification of the West Coast main line as far as Manchester the three WR sets were joined by the two six-car sets that had been new to the LMR, but by the end of 1973 all five (by now TOPS Class 251) would be withdrawn, their demise the result of poor reliability and a reputation for rough-riding — a problem that was never really solved. *Michael Mensing*

The BR Swindon-built 'Cross-country' sets (Class 120) were introduced in October 1957. There were 130 power cars, each fitted with two six-cylinder AEC or Leyland engines of 150hp (giving a total output per unit of 600hp), and 64 trailers. They entered service without four-character headcode displays, these being added later (and subsequently removed). Here a three-car set, with DMS(L) leading, leaves Templecombe for Kingswear on 5 March 1966. *Gavin Morrison*

In 1955 Park Royal Vehicles Ltd obtained an order to build 20 two-car units (later Class 103), each having two six-cylinder AEC engines of 150hp. They were introduced in 1957, mainly in the West Midlands; this unit is seen on 26 May 1966 working the 17.15 Rugby–Birmingham New Street service near Berkswell & Balsall Common. The picture was taken about half a mile east of Berkswell station and shows DTC(L) No M56162 leading. The class was not included in BR's DMU-refurbishment programme, the first set being withdrawn in the early 1970s, the last in February 1983. *Michael Mensing*

Built by the Sheffield firm of Cravens, the 50 two-car units that would later be known as the Class 112s and 113s were introduced in 1959 on services between St Pancras and Bedford. Fitted with two 238hp Rolls-Royce engines, they proved very troublesome, specifically as a result of the torque-converters overheating, and although 25 were rebuilt with standard mechanical transmission, in which form they proved more reliable, all had been withdrawn by November 1969. Here DMBS No 51690 is the leading vehicle of a set departing Bacup for Manchester on 3 December 1966, the last day of services on the branch. *Gavin Morrison*

*Above:* On 5 March 1967 a Gloucester RC&W (Class 100) two-car set, the leading vehicle recently ex works in early BR blue (a lighter shade than was finally adopted) with small yellow warning panel and red buffer-beams, leaves Hooton station, on the Wirral, for Helsby Junction. There were 40 of these two-car sets, powered by two BUT (AEC) 150hp engines; introduced to traffic from May 1957, they worked originally on the London Midland and Scottish Regions but were later transferred to the Eastern. Semi-lightweight units of steel construction, they were well built and gave good service, one lasting until 1989. *Gavin Morrison*

*Left:* A single-car Gloucester unit (Class 122) prepares to leave Penarth as the 12.05 shuttle to Cadoxton on 8 July 1967. *Hugh Ballantyne*

The Swindon-built 'Trans-Pennine' units (later Class 124) were visually different from most other types in that they had wrap-around cab windows, which looked extremely attractive. The fleet comprised 51 vehicles, built at Swindon and introduced on the Hull–Liverpool services via Standedge in January 1961. Based at Neville Hill, Leeds, the units consisted of six vehicles, four of them powered, the total of 1,840hp (produced by eight Leyland Albion six-cylinder engines of 230hp) being sufficient to deal easily with the gradients of the Pennines. On 8 July 1967 DMC No E51959 passes Diggle station (destined to close on 7 October 1968) before entering Standedge Tunnel. Many consider these to have been the most handsome of all the BR DMUs, and it is regrettable that none survived to be preserved. *Gavin Morrison*

*Left:* By now in BR blue, one of the original 'Derby Lightweights', DTC(L) No M79646 leading, departs Workington on 20 June 1968 as the 11.40am to Carlisle. *Michael Mensing*

*Below:* Built by BR at Derby, the sets that would later be known as the Class 108s were introduced in May 1958. Numbering 331 vehicles, of which 208 were powered (by two six-cylinder Leyland engines of 150hp), they ran in two-, three- or four-car formations. The final vehicle remained in service until 1993, and many survive into preservation. Here a two-car set in a mixed livery of blue and green catches the evening light on 1 April 1970 as it passes Rodley & Calverley on an Aire Valley working to Leeds, DMC(L) No E50638 leading. *Gavin Morrison*

*Below:* With headcode display filled in, a six-car Class 126 formation, with a DMBS(L) leading, passes Cadder Yard on a Glasgow–Edinburgh service. The photograph was taken on 16 May 1971, by which date most such workings on this route where in the hands of Class 27s 'topping and tailing' rakes of Mk 2 stock. *Derek Cross*

*Above:* Now painted in BR blue, a Class 110 'Calder Valley' set finds itself well away from its regular haunts whilst working a West Riding Railway Correspondence & Travel Society special on 9 September 1972. It is seen at Consett, having visited Redmire earlier in the day. *Gavin Morrison*

*Below:* Looking rather drab in plain BR blue, a Class 126 DMS(L) heads an Ayr–Glasgow train along the shore of Kilbernie Loch near Beith on a fine 22 July 1973. *Derek Cross*

*Left:* With the Pennine Hills as a backdrop, a Trans-Pennine Class 124 descends the 1-in-105 gradient from Marsden to Huddersfield on a working to Hull on 16 March 1974. The sets had by this date been reduced to five vehicles, the eight buffet cars having been withdrawn in 1972. *Gavin Morrison*

*Below:* An unusual combination on a Hull–Liverpool express on 14 May 1974, with a BRCW Class 104 vehicle heading a Swindon Trans-Pennine Class 124. The train is heading west past Heaton Lodge Junction, just to the west of Mirfield, where up trains used to take this track under the ex-Lancashire & Yorkshire lines. *Gavin Morrison*

Built by Metro-Cammell and introduced in 1957, what became known as Class 111 consisted of 50 driving motor cars and 24 intermediate trailers. The former were fitted with two six-cylinder 180hp Rolls-Royce engines, but in appearance they were almost identical to the Class 101s, their principle distinguishing feature being a four-character headcode display. Here an unidentified set headed by a DMC(L) in plain blue (and with Class 104 centre trailer) leaves Skipton on the 2.32pm to Leeds City on 13 September 1975. The last Class 111s would be withdrawn in 1989. *Michael Mensing*

Today a terminus, where trains from Middlesbrough reverse before continuing their journey to Whitby, Battersby was once a busy railway centre with lines from Middlesbrough, Whitby, Rosedale and Picton, on the Northallerton–Stockton route. With Newcastle on the destination board a Class 101 unit is seen departing on 28 June 1975. The steam visible above the rear coach is coming from Class K1 2-6-0 No 2005, based nearby on the North Yorkshire Moors Railway. *Gavin Morrison*

The sets that later became known as the Class 109s were built by D. Wickham & Co, of Ware, Hertfordshire, and introduced in August 1957 for use on the Eastern Region. Of lightweight construction, they proved susceptible to accident damage and were very expensive to repair. As there were only five sets built, they soon came to be regarded as non-standard, and some were withdrawn as early as September 1961. In 1967 DMBS No 50415 and DTC(L) No 56171 were converted for use by the General Manager of the Eastern Region, being renumbered DB975005 and DB975006, and are seen here in the yard next to York depot on 3 July 1975; note the cast-aluminium BR arrow — probably the only one ever affixed to a DMU. The set survives today in preservation on the Llangollen Railway. *Gavin Morrison*

Headed by DTS No E50883, a Class 116 formation leaves King's Cross on a suburban working on 10 July 1976. The Derby-built Class 116s were high-density units for suburban services, with a door to each bay and cramped seating; there were no toilet facilities and no connections between coaches. Introduced from 1957 and ultimately numbering 216 power cars and 104 trailers, they were allocated initially to the Western Region. The class was included in the DMU-refurbishment programme initiated in the 1970s, during the course of which some sets were fitted with toilets and corridor connections within sets, seating capacity being reduced accordingly. The last vehicles survived into the mid-1990s. *Gavin Morrison*

*Left:* Built at Derby in 1956, what became known as the Class 114 sets were the first to have the three-window raked-back front end. Pictured on 29 July 1976, DTC(L) No E56023 is the leading vehicle of a set departing Woodhouse station, on the outskirts of Sheffield, *en route* to Lincoln. Both vehicles appear to be recently ex works. *Gavin Morrison*

*Below:* A two-car Class 105 catches the winter sunlight inside York station on 20 November 1976. DTC(L) No 56440 is at the rear as the unit prepares to depart for the south. Built by the Cravens Railway Carriage & Wagon Co and introduced in 1956, these units were fitted with AEC six-cylinder 150hp engines. There were also three-car sets, as well as the Class 106s which were identical but for the fact that they had Leyland engines. *Gavin Morrison*

Class 122 Gloucester single car No M55003, in plain BR blue, arrives at King's Norton station on 21 May 1977. At this time there were four workings per day to/from Redditch; in 2010 there are two per hour on the electrified service between 6.30am and 23.00. *Michael Mensing*

The Class 108s were included in the BR
refurbishment programme in the late 1970s, and
initially the refurbished units were painted in
this attractive (but somewhat impractical) livery
of white with a blue stripe. A six-car formation
led by a two-car set leaves York for Leeds in
fine evening light on 30 April 1977.
*Gavin Morrison*

The Class 127s introduced in May 1959 were
high-capacity units with basic facilities (*i.e.*
one toilet per set, accessible only from the trailer
coach so equipped). They were a stopgap
measure pending electrification of the
St Pancras–Bedford services, as envisaged in the
1955 Modernisation Plan, but this was of low
priority, and the DMUs lasted around 22 years.
They had powerful eight-cylinder 238hp Rolls-
Royce engines and hydraulic transmission
but were not reliable and caused their
maintenance depot at Cricklewood a lot of
trouble. Framed by the signal gantries and
signalboxes at Brent Junction, near
Cricklewood, an eight-car set heads north for
Bedford on 21 May 1977. Following the
introduction in 1984 of the Class 317 EMUs,
22 of the 30 units, reduced to twin-sets, were
converted for parcels and newspaper traffic,
surviving in this form until 1989.
*Gavin Morrison*

Besides the three-car Hampshire' sets the
Southern Region's early DEMUs included the
six-car units built to the narrow body profile of
the Hastings line, the '6S' (later Class 201) and
'6L' (Class 202) sets of 1957 being followed in
1958 by seven '6Bs' (Class 203), each with a
buffet car in place of a TS. In all cases the
DMBS vehicles (two per unit) were each
equipped with two 500hp English Electric
4SRKT engines, giving a total power output of
2,000hp per unit. Seen at Waterloo on 27 August
1977 is Class 203 No 1035, with DMBS
No S60040 leading. The buffet vehicles were
withdrawn in 1980, reducing the Class 203s to
five-car units. *Michael Mensing*

*Left:* Bound for Bedford on 23 April 1978, a Class 127 emerges from the magnificent trainshed at St Pancras — a sight that has since been consigned to history. *Gavin Morrison*

*Below:* Between June 1977 and May 1979 the Class 123s were transferred to Hull Botanic Gardens for Trans-Pennine services, on which they continued, working with the Class 124s, until withdrawn in May 1984. This photograph, taken on 12 July 1979 at the south end of Selby station, features the unusual combination of Class 123 DMS(K) No E52103, with only one trailer car, coupled to a refurbished Metro-Cammell Class 101. The train is an afternoon Hull–Manchester working. *Gavin Morrison*

In the late 1970s certain Swindon Class 120 'Cross-Country' sets were dedicated to working the Central Wales line between Shrewsbury and Swansea, these units being easily identifiable by the spotlight mounted between the two front cab windows. Here Cardiff-based set No C612, with DMBC No W50712 leading, is passing Baston Hill as the 15.41 Shrewsbury–Swansea on 22 September 1979. The journey would take around 3½ hours. *Gavin Morrison*

With all the multi-coloured DMU liveries that are around in 2010 it is easy to forget that 30 years ago the situation was very different. Among the very few variations from the plain BR blue were the white stripe on the sides of the Class 104 units used mainly on Manchester Victoria–Blackpool services and the white cab roofs on the '104s' on Manchester Piccadilly–Buxton services. Introduced from 1957, what later became known as Class 104 numbered more than 300 vehicles built by the Birmingham Railway Carriage & Wagon Co.
On 28 September 1979 DMBS No M50475 leads a formation departing Bolton on a Blackpool–Manchester Victoria working. The best examples of this class were to last into the 1990s, despite being omitted from BR's refurbishment programme. *Gavin Morrison*

Painted in the mainly white livery applied to refurbished DMUs, Plymouth-based Class 116 set No P319 (with DMBS No W50868 leading) is seen about to draw into Exeter Central station after completing the 1-in-37 climb from St Davids. The date is 5 April 1980. *Gavin Morrison*

Also painted in the short-lived 'refurbished' livery is Class 101 DMBS No E50226, bringing up the rear of a two-car formation passing Wortley Junction on its way to Leeds City on 30 July 1980. In the background, passing the site of the erstwhile LNWR's Copley Hill goods yard, can be seen another Class 101 on a Leeds–Huddersfield service. The line just visible in the immediate foreground, forming the third side of the Copley Hill triangle, is part of the direct route from Wakefield Westgate to Bradford Interchange. *Gavin Morrison*

*Left:* Repainted in BR blue and grey following refurbishment, a Class 114 Derby 'heavyweight' set, with DMBS No E50009 leading, works the New Holland Pier–Cleethorpes service on 12 June 1981. The line opened in March 1848 but by the date of this picture was just two weeks from closure — a consequence of the opening of the Humber road bridge. The ferry service was operated by a diesel-powered paddle vessel, the *Farringford*, built in 1947 for the Lymington–Yarmouth service. *Gavin Morrison*

*Below:* With DMBS No W51406 bringing up the rear, WR Class 117 set No L426 approaches Hereford station from the north on 13 June 1981. *Gavin Morrison*

*Below:* With DMBC No W51074 leading, refurbished WR Class 119 three-car set No C595 approaches Weston-super-Mare as the 15.00 ex Bristol Temple Meads on 31 March 1982. *Michael Mensing*

*Below right:* Class 101 DMBS No E50224 arrives at Clayton West on 14 November 1982 at the head of the 12.10 service from Huddersfield. To the right of the signalbox can be seen Emley Moor mast, built 1969-71 and 1,084ft tall, the top being 1,939ft above sea level. The previous mast (1,266ft) collapsed on 19 March 1969. Opened in September 1879, the 3½-mile Clayton West branch left the Huddersfield–Penistone line at Clayton West Junction. Passenger services were withdrawn on 22 January 1983, and the branch closed completely in October of that year. The 15in-gauge Kirklees Light Railway, opened as a tourist line in 1991, operates over four miles of the old trackbed. *Gavin Morrison*

*Right:* In the summer of 1983 the Class 124s, along with the Class 123s, were still employed on Manchester Piccadilly–Hull/Cleethorpes workings via the Hope Valley, albeit reduced to four cars. The Trans-Pennine logo is clearly visible on the side of the DMC as a formation climbs out of Sheffield, passing Millhouses, on 13 August. At this date the units were also used on Hull–Lancaster diagrams. *Gavin Morrison*

*Below:* Awaiting its next duty, a very smart Class 105 Cravens two-car set stands in the yard at Ipswich station on 12 April 1984. Nearer the camera is DMBS No E51291, with headcode panel removed; the other vehicle is a DTC(L). *Gavin Morrison*

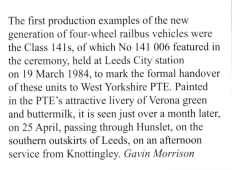

The first production examples of the new generation of four-wheel railbus vehicles were the Class 141s, of which No 141 006 featured in the ceremony, held at Leeds City station on 19 March 1984, to mark the formal handover of these units to West Yorkshire PTE. Painted in the PTE's attractive livery of Verona green and buttermilk, it is seen just over a month later, on 25 April, passing through Hunslet, on the southern outskirts of Leeds, on an afternoon service from Knottingley. *Gavin Morrison*

*Left:* On 26 April 1984 a Class 123 formation, DMBS(L) No E52089 leading, passes New Mills Junction and takes the route via Marple and Romiley to Manchester Piccadilly on a Trans-Pennine working. These units were replaced later in the year by locomotive-hauled trains, which ran via the Hope Valley to Hull and Cleethorpes. *Gavin Morrison*

*Below:* By the spring of 1984 the BRCW Class 104 units were being used to help out on rush-hour services between Manchester and Hayfield or Glossop, hitherto the preserve of Class 506 electric units. On 27 April renumbered DMC No 53496 (formerly 50496) passes the signalbox at Dinting, on the direct Hayfield–Manchester side of the triangle. *Gavin Morrison*

A commanding view of Shrewsbury station, recorded on 18 August 1984 from the famous Severn Bridge signalbox. A Class 120 Swindon Cross-Country set is arriving from the Birmingham line with DMS(L) No 53679 at the rear a Class 101 trailer in the middle. In the distance is another Class 120 set, the spotlight between the cab windows identifying it as one of those dedicated to the Central Wales service. On the right is Class 47/4 No 47 479 waiting to depart for Paddington. *Gavin Morrison*

Only two Class 210 DEMUs were constructed, at BREL York and Derby in 1981/2. They were built as prototypes, one for long-distance work and the other fitted out for shorter workings. They were built to the body design already adopted for the Class 317 and 455 EMUs and had compatibility between the types as far as speed, coupling and braking systems. They varied from the usual DMU concept in that the two-car set (No 210 001) was fitted with a 1,125hp Paxman 6RP200L engine, whilst the three-car set (210 002) was powered by a 1,140hp 12-cylinder MTU 12V396 TC12 engine, both with diesel-electric transmission, both units having above-floor-mounted engines. The sets were allocated to Reading for primarily working to Paddington. Apparently they performed well and were liked by the crews, but in 1987 they returned to Derby RTC, where some of the vehicles saw further use. No 210 002 is shown ready to leave Paddington on 1 November 1984 as the 15.04 all-stations to Reading. *Colin J. Marsden*

*Above:* In the early 1970s a Park Royal Class 103 set, comprising DMBS(L) No 50396 and DTC(L) No 56162, was converted for use by the Railway Technical Centre at Derby and painted in the latter's distinctive livery. By now given carriage numbers 975089/90 and known as Laboratory Coach No 5, it is seen passing Clay Cross Junction as it returns to Derby as special working 2Z24 on 14 March 1985. *Gavin Morrison*

*Right:* Away from its usual duties in the Welsh Valleys, WR Cardiff-area set No C307, complete with Welsh Dragon logo on the cab end, is seen at Crewe station on 1 June 1985. The leading vehicle is Class 116 DMBS No W53820, while the intermediate trailer is Class 101 TC(L) No W59550. *Gavin Morrison*

Still operating as a three-car unit on 1 June 1985, a refurbished Class 110 'Calder Valley' set in BR blue/grey livery approaches Sowerby Bridge station on a service to Manchester Victoria. On the skyline can be seen the famous Wainhouse Tower, a folly built in 1875 by the eccentric Edward Wainhouse — allegedly so that he could see into his next-door neighbour's garden. A very fine structure, with 403 steps to climb to the top, it is open to the public only occasionally. *Gavin Morrison*

Built in 1981, Class 140 No 140 001 was the prototype which eventually resulted in the construction of the Class 141s and 'Pacer' units. During the course of its trials it travelled extensively over the network for many years, being seen here jacked up on sleepers and with wheels removed at the back of Plymouth Laira shed on 24 August 1985; no doubt its presence influenced the allocation here of 'Pacers' (one of which can be seen on the right of the picture) for use in Cornwall. A year later it was at Leeds Holbeck, stored for some time before eventually being preserved at the Keith & Dufftown Railway, where it arrived in 1994. *Gavin Morrison*

In 1985, when BR blue and grey was still very much the order of the day, Plymouth-based BRCW Class 118 set No P460 caused quite a stir by appearing in this bright-yellow advertising livery for British Telecom. With DMS No 51317 nearest the camera, it is pictured in the siding alongside the main line at Laira on 24 August. *Gavin Morrison*

In 1985 two distinctive-looking Class 151 units were built by Metro-Cammell to rival the Class 150s and were extensively tested, usually on routes based at Derby. They had Cummins NT855 285hp engines with Twin Disc 1330 hydraulic 'hot shift' gearboxes and were capable of a maximum speed of 75mph. With Class 31/4 No 31 454 in the background, No 151 002 is seen leaving Doncaster for Sheffield on 27 April 1986. The '151s' would be withdrawn in March 1989. *Gavin Morrison*

*Left:* Following withdrawal from service in 1977 a Class 100 set consisting of DMBS No E51122 and DTS(L) No E56300 was converted for use by the Eastern Region's General Manager, the vehicles adopting Departmental carriage numbers DB975664 and DB975637 respectively. In immaculate external condition, as might be expected, it is pictured on 22 May 1986 heading south on the goods lines to the south of Doncaster near Bridge Junction. *Gavin Morrison*

*Below:* Painted in Red Star livery, Class 128 MLV No 55994 approaches Sutton Bridge Junction, off the Cambrian main line, on 7 June 1986. Note the black section between the two windows, the former gangway connection having been removed. *Gavin Morrison*

In 1984 a Class 114 set, consisting of DMBS No 53045 and DTS(L) No 54004, was painted experimentally in South Yorkshire PTE colours of brown and cream. It was photographed on 27 June 1986 well away from its intended area of operation, at Bradford Interchange, about to tackle the 1-in-50 gradient to Laisterdyke on its journey to Leeds. *Gavin Morrison*

The Buxton-allocated Class 108 three-car sets were painted with white cab roofs. Here two sets, with DMBS No 51395 leading, are seen at Frodsham, working a summer-Saturday Llandudno–Manchester train on 23 August 1986. *Gavin Morrison*

Bristol-area Class 117 set No B430, comprising DMBS No 51368, TC(L) No 59520 and DMS No 51410, was repainted in this chocolate-and-cream livery for the GWR150 celebrations in 1985. It is seen leaving Severn Tunnel Junction for Newport on 2 March 1987, at which time this location was still a busy centre for freight traffic. *Gavin Morrison*

*Above:* Prior to the introduction of Class 158 'Express' units Trans-Pennine services were occasionally worked by new Class 150/2 'Sprinters' operating in multiple. Here, on 12 April 1987, No 150 226 heads a six-car formation passing Longwood, on the 1-in-105 climb from Huddersfield to Standedge Tunnel. The train is the 09.51 York–Liverpool. Note that the cab front is devoid of yellow save on the connecting door — a feature that was to be very short-lived. *Gavin Morrison*

*Below:* This unique livery, promoting the Scottish Highlands and Islands and featuring prominently the 'Highland terrier' motif used by Eastfield depot, was applied in 1985 to Class 104 No 104 325. Nicknamed the 'Mexican Bean', it was based at Oban, where it had one regular diagram each week to Crianlarich and back on a Sunday evening; otherwise its main use was to cover for locomotive failures. In this photograph, taken at Crianlarich Upper on 28 June 1987, the DTC(L) is leading, and DMBS No 53434 (formerly No 50434) is on the rear. Note the headlight on the cab roof. *Gavin Morrison*

The first production 'Sprinters' were the Class 150/1s, two-car sets built at BREL York in 1985/6. Wearing the original Provincial Sector livery, the first of many schemes that would be applied to the class over the years, No 150 112 is seen passing Gaer Junction while working a Birmingham–Cardiff service on 4 August 1987. In the background are the old and new Newport Tunnels (also called Hillfield), respectively 748yd and 770yd long. *Gavin Morrison*

Painted in GWR-style chocolate and cream and based at Plymouth Laira for use on branch lines in Devon and Cornwall, 'Pacer' No 142 022 waits to leave Par for Penzance on 28 August 1987. Known locally as 'Skippers', on account of their rough riding, these units were not ideally suited to the tight curves of these branches, resulting in damage to the track and to wheelsets, and later in the year they were transferred north to Yorkshire. *Gavin Morrison*

The Class 110 'Calder Valley' units were ousted from their Trans-Pennine duties in the late 1980s as various 'Sprinters' and 'Super Sprinters' became available to take over the Leeds–Bradford–Manchester route. By now in 'power-twin' configuration, and with DMBC leading, one of the displaced sets leaves Rotherham on an evening Sheffield–York service on 25 July 1988. *Gavin Morrison*

Well away from its regular stamping-ground, Class 144 No 144 006, in the later West Yorkshire PTE livery of red and cream , passes Friargate Crossing, near Grimsby, on 23 February 1989. *Gavin Morrison*

*Left:* In Network SouthEast days the Class 121s were employed regularly on services between West Ealing and Greenford. No 55028 is pictured departing West Ealing on 15 April 1989. *Gavin Morrison*

*Below:* On 13 May 1989 a seven-car DMU formation, with Class 108 DMBS No 51935 leading, finds itself in unusual surroundings as it passes Beckfoot, near Low Gill, before tackling the climb to Shap on a special from Lancashire to Carlisle. *Gavin Morrison*

*Above:* On 18 May 1989 a three-car Class 119 in Network SouthEast livery arrives at Didcot Parkway station as the 15.26 Oxford–Reading. *Michael Mensing*

*Right:* On a perfect summer's day (22 June 1989) and with the Tay Bridge in the background, Provincial Sector-liveried Class 150/2s Nos 150 208 and 150 262 head south past Wormit as the 16.52 Dundee–Edinburgh. The '150/2s' worked the Fife Circle and Edinburgh–Dundee services for many years until supplanted *c*2004 by Class 158s and 170/4s. *Gavin Morrison*

Painted in the orange livery of Strathclyde PTE, a Class 107 (set No 107 726 in the series introduced latterly by the Scottish Region) makes the 1-in-41 descent of Cowlairs Bank towards Glasgow Queen Street on 4 July 1989. Bringing up the rear is DMC(L) No 52018. *Gavin Morrison*

*Right:* Repainted in the very smart Royal Mail livery of Post Office red with yellow ends and doors, Class 128 DMLV No 55995 rounds the chord from Salford Crescent to Ordsall Lane on its way to Manchester Piccadilly on 23 July 1989. The last of these vehicles would be retired after service on 12 October 1990. *Gavin Morrison*

*Below:* Modified with roller blinds and looking extremely smart in Royal Mail livery, a Class 108, DMBS No 55931 leading, approaches Paddington on 4 October 1989. Just visible on the right of the picture is Class 117 DMBS No 51337, in Network SouthEast colours. *Gavin Morrison*

The Class 158s, known as 'Express Sprinters', were built at BREL Derby in the period 1989-92. In all 182 units were built, of which 17 were three-car sets for Trans-Pennine services, the remainder being two-car. They were numbered 158 701-872 and 158 901-10 (these last being for West Yorkshire PTE). All were fitted with Cummins 350hp NTA855RL engines, except for Nos 158 815-62, which had 350hp Perkins 2006-TW11s, and 158 863-72, which received 400hp Cummins NTA 855R3 engines for use mainly on the Manchester–Cardiff route. All were capable of 90mph, and over the years they have been seen as far afield as Penzance, Wick, Holyhead, Fishguard and Hull, as well as at most places in between. The picture shows a brand-new No 158 722 ready for delivery from Derby on 2 March 1990. *Gavin Morrison*

The second of the Class 150 prototypes was fitted originally with Rolls-Royce engines and Self Changing Gears fully automatic transmission. These had given problems, so in 1986 the unit was chosen to serve as a testbed for the forthcoming Class 158s, being fitted with air-conditioning equipment, uprated Cummins engines and, on one vehicle, an improved version of the twin-disc torque-converter transmission fitted originally to the Class 151 prototypes. Renumbered 154 002 and photographed thus at Derby on 16 March 1990, it would later revert to its original identity as Class 150 No 150 002. *Gavin Morrison*

*Right:* Immaculate in Network SouthEast livery, an ex-works Class 108 headed by DMBS No 51916 draws into Woburn Sands station while working a Bedford–Bletchley service on 20 March 1990. *Gavin Morrison*

*Below:* Class 115 DMBS No 51885 calls at Little Kemble on 20 March 1990 at the head of an afternoon Princes Risborough–Aylesbury working. *Gavin Morrison*

*Right:* Prior to the 'Express' units came the 'Super Sprinters' of Classes 155 (built by Leyland) and 156 (Metro-Cammell). The former were very much in the minority, numbering just 35 two-car units (plus a further seven for West Yorkshire PTE), among them No 155 328, photographed on 28 September 1990 from the bridge that leads to Cardiff Canton shed, to the west of the station. *Gavin Morrison*

*Below:* No further units of the Metro-Cammell Class 151 design were ordered, and by 4 February 1991, when this photograph was taken, both were stored in the old carriage sheds at Llandudno Junction. There followed a further period in store at the Railway Technical Centre at Derby, which came to an end in March 2000 when the units were sold to Railtest (later Serco). Both would be cut up at Crewe in 2004. *Gavin Morrison*

*Above right:* The Class 143s, built in 1985/6, were similar in concept to the '142s' but had bodywork built by Alexander on Barclay frames. They were allocated originally to the North East, where some gained Tyne & Wear PTE livery, one being seen on 24 June 1991 at Cargo Fleet, Middlesbrough, on a Saltburn–Darlington service. The class now operates mainly in South Wales. *Gavin Morrison*

*Right:* A Network SouthEast service from Aylesbury to Marylebone draws into Amersham station on 5 July 1991. The unit is a Class 115 four-car set (one of 41, built at Derby between March and December 1960), which type monopolised services out of Marylebone until replaced in the early 1990s by Class 165/0 'Turbostar' units. *Gavin Morrison*

Photographed from the town's by-pass road, Network SouthEast-liveried Class 101 set No L700 approaches King's Lynn on 14 September 1991. However, all is not what it might seem: the line here was singled and electrified in 1990, and the '101', based at Old Oak Common, was working a special in connection with a Network SouthEast open weekend, during which locomotive-hauled passenger trains were run on the Middleton Towers branch. *Gavin Morrison*

Additional to the 35 Class 155 units for Regional Railways were seven funded by West Yorkshire PTE and delivered in 1988. Still in its original livery, which it retained for around 18 years, No 155 341 is pictured departing Leeds for Bradford Interchange on 28 February 1992. All seven are still based at Neville Hill depot and are usually employed on Leeds–Bradford–Manchester Victoria services, operated nowadays by Northern. *Gavin Morrison*

About 1½ miles from Aberdare on the Merthyr line in South Wales is Cwmbach, where Regional Railways-liveried Class 143 No 143 621 was photographed on 15 April 1992 on a Cardiff–Barry Island service. *Gavin Morrison*

Introduced by the Southern Region in 1962 were the 19 three-car DEMUs of Class 3D, better known as the 'Oxted' units and in later years as Class 207. A development of the earlier '3H' (Class 205), the design was readily identifiable by the recesses for the cables and sockets on the cab fronts. Four First-class compartments were provided in the centre trailer, the rest of the set consisting open Second-class bays. There was only one lavatory, in the centre trailer, and the lack of gangway connections mean that this could not be reached from the other vehicles. Traditionally associated with secondary lines in Surrey and East Sussex, they could latterly be found further afield, set No 207 013, by now in Network SouthEast livery, being seen heading a down service away from Andover station on 29 April 1992. *Gavin Morrison*

Bound for Manchester Piccadilly and Buxton and with the cooling towers of Kearsley power station (since demolished) as a backdrop, Class 150/1 No 150 136 passes Agecroft on 25 June 1992. Painted in the later Greater Manchester PTE livery, it is running as a three-car set, the centre vehicle being a DMBS from a Class 150/2. *Gavin Morrison*

In the attractive orange livery adopted originally by Greater Manchester PTE, 'Pacer' No 142 012 passes Thorpes Bridge Junction, heading towards Rochdale on what is probably an Oldham-loop working, on 26 August 1993. The line branching off to the right used to lead to Manchester Victoria via Red Bank but has since been closed. About half a mile in arrear of the road bridge from which the photograph was taken is Newton Heath depot. *Gavin Morrison*

Still in its original Provincial Sector livery on 23 October 1993, Class 142 No 142 091 arrives at Penistone on a Sheffield–Huddersfield working. Class 142 was a development of Class 141 and numbered 96 units built by BREL Derby in the years 1985-7. At the time of writing all but one survive; most operate in the North of England, the remainder in the Welsh Valleys or in Devon. *Gavin Morrison*

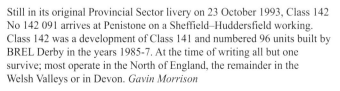

Eggborough power station dominates the skyline as Class 141 No 141 107, in West Yorkshire PTE livery, passes Whitley Bridge Junction on a mid-day Leeds–Snaith working on 26 April 1994. The class was not entirely successful, and the two- and three-car sets were withdrawn by 1997. A number were exported to Iran, but No 141 113 is preserved at Weardale Railway. *Gavin Morrison*

The first 14 units of Class 142 were allocated to Newton Heath depot for Greater Manchester PTE services. On 16 July 1994 No 142 008, in the second livery adopted by the PTE, heads along the Liverpool–Warrington side of the triangle at Earlstown. At the time of writing this is the only member of the class to have been withdrawn, as a result of severe accident damage sustained at Winsford South Junction on 23 June 1999, when it was hit in the rear by Class 87 No 87 027 *Wolf of Badenoch*, working a down Virgin express. *Gavin Morrison*

In 1994 Class 101 unit No 101 685 was repainted in an approximation of its original BR green livery, with half-yellow front end. Consisting of DMS(L) No 53160, TS(L) No 59359 and DMBS No 51364, it was based at Longsight, Manchester, but in the 1990s could usually be found working along the North Wales coast. Here, on 10 September 1994, it is seen leaving Glas Conwy on an afternoon Blaenau Ffestiniog–Llandudno working. *Gavin Morrison*

The Class 144s were built in 1986/7 by BREL Derby with Alexander bodies for services in Yorkshire, where the entire class of 23 two- and three-car units has always been concentrated. Here No 144 013, in Regional Railways livery, pauses at Hensall while *en route* from Goole to Leeds service on 23 March 1995. The old station house in the background is nowadays a private dwelling but has many interesting railway items on show. *Gavin Morrison*

*Above:* Only five Class 150/2s received Merseyrail's colour scheme of yellow with a black stripe, known to some as 'bumble bee' livery. No 150 205 is shown approaching Bolton station from the east on an evening commuter working on 26 April 1995. *Gavin Morrison*

By now in Centro (West Midlands PTE) livery, prototype Class 150 No 150 001, a three-car unit, waits to depart Liverpool Lime Street ready for Crewe on 13 May 1995. Over the years the Class 150/0 and 150/1 units, lacking through corridor connections, have generally been allocated to the North West and Midlands, although some have worked for Silverlink. *Gavin Morrison*

Smartly repainted in Regional Railways livery, Class 101 set No 101 682, consisting of DMBS No 53256 and DMS(L) No 51505, calls at Betws-y-Coed on a working to Blaenau Ffestiniog on 13 August 1995. On the right of the picture can be seen the miniature railway layout at the railway museum. *Gavin Morrison*

The 114 Class 156 two-car 'Super Sprinters' were built at Metro-Cammell's Washwood Heath, Birmingham, plant in the years 1987-9. The first examples were based originally at Norwich, but operation of the type soon spread to the Midlands, North Wales North West, North East and Scotland. This picture, taken on 27 April 1998, shows No 156 512, in the original Strathclyde livery, passing through the colourful gorse bushes near Prestwick golf course as the 18.42 Govan–Kilmarnock. *Gavin Morrison*

Over the years the Class 156 units have worn many liveries, the first being that of Regional Railways, seen here on No 156 477 *Highland Festival*, leaving Brora on 25 May 1998 as the 07.00 Inverness–Thurso. *Gavin Morrison*

*Above:* Built by BREL as Class 158s but converted at Rosyth Dockyard before entering service, the 22 Class 159 units were introduced by Network SouthEast to replace locomotive haulage on services between Waterloo and Exeter. Forming the 10.00

Brighton–Paignton, Nos 159 002 *City of Salisbury* and 159 017 are seen passing the well-known location of Horse Cove, between Dawlish and Teignmouth, on 15 August 1998. *Gavin Morrison*

*Below:* Sellafield nuclear power station dominates this picture of 'Pacer' No 142 056 departing as the 16.40 to Barrow on 26 August 1998. Livery is Merseyrail yellow with black stripe. *Gavin Morrison*

*Above:* Introduced in May 1958, the single cars built by the Gloucester Railway Carriage & Wagon Co and fitted with two AEC six-cylinder 150hp engines operated initially on the Western Region. In later years, however, they were to be seen elsewhere on the network, and in the early 1990s No 55012 passed to Loadhaul (the North Eastern part of the erstwhile Railfreight operation) for route learning. Repainted in the striking Loadhaul livery of dark grey and orange, it is seen passing Stainforth, heading for Doncaster, on 23 February 1999. *Gavin Morrison*

*Above right:* Upon privatisation Class 158 units Nos 158 752-9 found themselves allocated to North West Trains, being employed principally on services from North Wales to Crewe and Manchester. No 158 752, yet to receive the 'gold star' embellishments, is pictured approaching Llandudno Junction on 1 April 1999 as the 12.06 from Manchester. These eight sets have since been strengthened to three cars and are used nowadays on Northern services between Blackpool and York. *Gavin Morrison*

*Below:* Twenty-one three-car Class 166s were built by ABB at York in 1992/3. They were known as 'Network Express Turbos' and 'Thames Turbos', as they were used by Network SouthEast on the Thames Valley services. They passed into the Thames Trains franchise. They have Perkins 2006-TW11 engines with a 90mph capability, and are also fitted with AWS and TPWS. Still in NSE livery on 2 July 1999, No 166 207 heads a six-car formation calling at Twyford *en route* to Paddington from Henley. In 2004 the Thames Trains franchise was amalgamated with that of Great Western. *Gavin Morrison*

The Class 165/0 units were constructed at BREL at York in 1990/1. The build comprised 20 two- and 17 three-car sets, each car being fitted with a 350hp Perkins 2006-TW11 engine, giving a top speed of 75mph. They became known as 'Networker Turbos' when introduced by Network SouthEast for the Chiltern-line services, on which they replaced the Class 115s. Still in NSE livery, unit No 165 009 heads north from Banbury on a service to Birmingham on 10 July 1999. *Gavin Morrison*

Built by Adtranz at Derby, the five Class 168/0 'Clubman' units were the first DMUs ordered following railway privatisation. Capable of a maximum speed of 100mph, they entered service in 1997, on Chiltern Railways services between Marylebone and Birmingham.
No 168 002 is seen approaching Tyseley on a down express on 10 July 1999. *Gavin Morrison*

At the start of the 21st century three of the Class 121 single cars, built by Pressed Steel and introduced in 1960, remained in use with Silverlink on Bedford–Bletchley services. Superbly maintained by Bletchley depot, they often worked in pairs. This picture, taken at Stewartby on 24 July 1999, features the 09.56 from Bletchley, formed by No 55027 (unit No 121 017) in Silverlink livery and named *Bletchley TMD* and No 55031 (121 031) *Leslie Crabbe* in Network SouthEast colours. *Gavin Morrison*

*Left:* In 1999 Wales & West had on its books no fewer than 39 Class 158s, including the batch of 10 (Nos 158 863-72) fitted with 400hp Cummins NTA855R3 engines. Pictured ready to depart Newport for Cardiff on 1 October, No 158 867 was the only one to receive this experimental version of Alphaline livery. *Gavin Morrison*

*Below:* On 6 November 1999 a Rugby World Cup special, believed to have originated from Sleaford and consisting of Centro-liveried units Nos 150 214 and 150 105, passes St Brides, between Newport and Cardiff. The Rugby World Cup produced at least 11 specials, plus locomotive-hauled services from the Valleys, and many other trains had coaches added. *Gavin Morrison*

ScotRail operates the largest fleet of 'Turbostars', comprising 59 three-car sets. Of these, 38 (including Nos 170 393-6, operated originally by Hull Trains) have First-class accommodation and mini-buffets and are used mainly on Glasgow–Edinburgh–Aberdeen–Inverness services. On 21 February 2002 No 170 403, in the very striking livery applied initially to those units that were new to ScotRail, races east past the site of Saughton Junction, where the routes to Glasgow Queen Street and Aberdeen diverge. *Gavin Morrison*

*Right:* Class 143 'Pacer' No 143 601, in Valley Lines livery, works a Gloucester–Taunton service near Creek St Michael in June 2001. *David Cable*

*Below:* In the spring of 2000 Central Trains had an allocation of 36 Class 158s based at Tyseley. All would eventually be painted in the attractive green livery seen here on No 158 790 as it takes the up slow line through the cutting at Barrow-on-Soar, between Loughborough and Leicester, on 6 May. *Gavin Morrison*

Class 166 No 166 206, in Thames Trains livery, slows for a stop at Slough while *en route* for Paddington on 2 July 2001. *Gavin Morrison*

The northern extremity of Britain's rail network is Wick, where on 21 August 2001 Class 158 No 158 734, in the attractive ScotRail livery, is seen ready to depart as the 16.17 to Inverness. Haymarket depot in Edinburgh was the first to receive these 'Express' units, in mid-1990, and at the time of writing still has an allocation, now used on more local services, although a number remain based at Inverness for services to Aberdeen and the Far North. *Gavin Morrison*

Bombardier's depot at Central Rivers, near Burton-upon-Trent, was purpose-built for the maintenance of the Class 220 'Voyagers' and 221 'Super Voyagers'. This picture was taken on the opening day, 18 September 2001, and shows Nos 220 017 and 220 002. Thirty-four non-tilting Class 220s were constructed, in 2000/1, each car being powered by a 750hp Cummins engine, giving 3,000hp per set, and allowing very rapid acceleration for a 185.6-ton train. The trains generated huge increases in passenger numbers for Virgin CrossCountry, which resulted in severe overcrowding on certain routes. *Gavin Morrison*

Heading for Nottingham on 8 December 2001, Class 156 No 156 402, in Regional Railways 'Express' livery, has just passed over the flat crossing with the East Coast main line north of Newark. The photograph was taken from a bridge over the Newark by-pass. *Gavin Morrison*

Bombardier Transportation took over the site of Procor (formerly Charles Roberts) at Horbury, near Wakefield, for the assembly of some of the Class 220 and 221 'Voyagers', the others being assembled in Brugge in Belgium. Seen in various stages of completion inside the works are various Class 221 'Super Voyagers' on 12 December 2001, the day the final 'Voyager', No 220 034 (later named *Yorkshire Voyager*) was handed over to Virgin. The 40 five-car Class 221s (along with the four four-car units), were built in 2001/2, each car being fitted with a Cummins 750hp engine, making a total of 3,750hp available to power the 281.9-ton train. These units were fitted with a tilt mechanism, with different bogies and control equipment from the Class 220s, and were known as 'Super Voyagers'. However, since 2008 the CrossCountry sets have had the tilt mechanism isolated, there being little opportunity to use it on the routes they serve, and it is expected that this action will result in even better availability figures. *Gavin Morrison*

In order to test its tilting capabilities the first of the Class 221 'Super Voyagers', No 221 101, was subjected to extensive trials on SNCF tracks through the mountainous region between Cahors and Brive, in central France, while high-speed trials were conducted between Brive and Le Mans. This rare photograph, taken on 1 February 2002, shows No 221 101 *Louis Bleriot* alongside an SNCF 'BB7xxx' electric locomotive at Brive, prior to leaving for Le Mans. *Gavin Morrison*

The view from inside the cab of Class 221 No 221 101 as the unit races between Cahors and Brive on 1 February 2002, showing the tilt in operation. *Gavin Morrison*

*Above:* A pair of Class 220s, Nos 220 017 *Bombardier Voyager* and 220 008 *Draig Gymreig / Welsh Dragon*, climb the short 1-in-75 gradient out of Holyhead as they leave on a special press trip on 16 March 2002. The Class 221 'Super Voyagers' are now used regularly on Euston–Holyhead services, whilst the Class 220s, now devoid of names, are allocated to CrossCountry. *Gavin Morrison*

*Below:* One of the 17 three-car Class 158s (Nos 158 798-814) in Northern Spirit Trans-Pennine livery, No 158 811 is seen inside Liverpool Lime Street station on 28 August 2002, waiting to leave as the 12.25 to Middlesbrough. Throughout Arriva's tenure of the franchise these units remained as three-car sets, but now that the Class 185 'Desiros' have taken over Trans-Pennine services the '158s' have been dispersed, some being transferred intact to South West Trains (eight, converted to Class 159/1, in exchange for Class 170/3 'Turbostars') or First Great Western (one) and the remainder reduced to two-car units for use by East Midlands Trains (five) or South West Trains (three), the intermediates being used to strengthen Northern sets Nos 158 752-9 on services between Blackpool and York. *Gavin Morrison*

This striking orange livery was one of a number of non-standard schemes used by Wales & West to promote the 'Heart of Wales' line. Single car No 153 303 is at the rear of Class 158 No 158 832, leaving Crewe for Manchester Piccadilly on the afternoon of 28 March 2002. Class 153 was created in 1991/2 by splitting the two-car Leyland-built Class 155 'Super Sprinters'. *Gavin Morrison*

Class 101 power-twin unit No 101 692, formed of DMS(L) No 53170 and DMBS No 532353, was unique in being painted in a special blue livery for Strathclyde PTE and was usually employed on the Cumbernauld services. When displaced from Scotland it was allocated to Longsight depot, from where it worked local services around Manchester. Still proclaiming allegiance to its former sponsor, it is pictured arriving at Manchester Piccadilly on 15 April 2002. *Gavin Morrison*

Wales & Borders Alphaline livery is displayed by Class 158 No 158 817 as it departs Crewe for Manchester Piccadilly on a working from South Wales on 11 May 2002. The unit is one of those fitted with a 350hp Perkins 2006-TW11 engine. *Gavin Morrison*

*Above:* Painted in Railtrack livery and with driving cars converted from a Class 101 set, a Class 960 ultrasonic testing/tractor unit, comprising No 977301 (built 1959) and No 977392 (built 1956) coupled either side of Track Assessment Unit No 999602, stands outside Ayr depot on 29 August 2002. *Gavin Morrison*

*Below:* On 8 September 2002 a very clean No 144 006, the first of its class to don the third style of West Yorkshire PTE livery, stands outside Neville Hill depot, Leeds. It was also the only '144' to receive the Metro 'M' logo on the front but ran with this embellishment for only a short period. *Gavin Morrison*

*Right:* In the autumn of 2002 North West Trains had eight Class 153 on its books. No 153 359, in rather drab blue livery, heads east out of Chester at 11.35 on 23 September. *Gavin Morrison*

*Below:* Heading north on the 07.20 Penzance– Glasgow service, an unidentified Class 220 'Voyager' of Virgin CrossCountry crosses the River Lune at Lancaster on 20 January 2003. *Gavin Morrison*

*Bottom:* Bound for Liverpool Street, three-car 'Turbostar' No 170 203, in Anglia livery, crosses Manningtree Viaduct on 21 February 2003. Anglia Railways ordered eight of these three-car sets, Nos 170 201-8, for the services from Liverpool Street to Norwich, Ipswich, Lowestoft and Bury St Edmunds. Between 2002 and 2004 four of these units were hired to Hull Trains. *Gavin Morrison*

*Above:* On 24 June 2003 Silverlink-liveried Class 150/1 No 150 120 calls at Ridgmont on the 12.17 Bletchley–Bedford service.
*Gavin Morrison*

*Below:* One of 11 Class 205 (mainly) three-car units to receive the yellow, blue and white colours of Connex SouthCentral was No 205 001, seen at Oxted station on 7 July 2003. *Jason Rogers*

By the summer of 2003 the colourful 'Visit Wales' promotional livery had been applied to Wales & Borders Class 150/2 No 150 281, here with Class 153 No 153 312 attached to the rear. The formation is pictured calling at Whitland station on a mid-day Pembroke Dock–Carmarthen service on 9 August. *Gavin Morrison*

In an attractive sky-blue livery with purple doors, Porterbrook spot-hire 'Turbostar' No 170 397, built in 2002, is advertising 'Q Jump', an online ticket-booking website. It is seen ready to depart from the north end of Coventry station on 12 September 2003. *Gavin Morrison*

After 47 years the career of the Class 101 Metropolitan-Cammell units came to an end on 21 December 2003. All the survivors were based at Longsight depot, which had managed to keep the best examples in service using parts removed from withdrawn units. A special was organised to mark the occasion, which consisted of sets 101 685 (BR green livery), 101 693 (Strathclyde PTE) and 101 676 (Regional Railways). Originating in Manchester and visiting Buxton and Barrow-in-Furness, it is shown at Ordsall Lane, Salford, on its journey north. *Gavin Morrison*

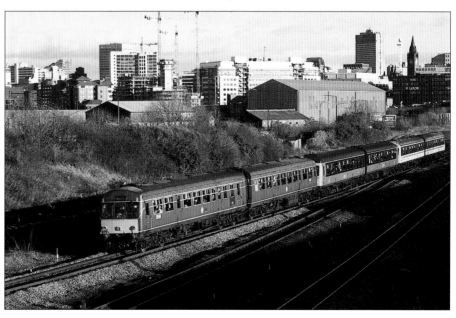

*Left:* The second livery adopted by Strathclyde PTE was known as carmine and cream (albeit featuring shades rather different from the BR carriage-stock livery of the early 1950s). Thus adorned, Class 156 No 156 510 is pictured on 22 March 2004 having just departed Gretna Green on the 09.53 Glasgow Central–Carlisle service via the Glasgow & South Western route. The single-line section between here and Annan has recently been restored to double track. *Gavin Morrison*

*Below:* A side-on view of Arriva-liveried Class 153 No 153 378 passing Mauds Bridge, between Thorne and Scunthorpe, on a working to Doncaster on 13 April 2004. *Gavin Morrison*

Only four Class 142s (Nos 142 023/50/65/6) received Northern Spirit livery, retaining this throughout Arriva's tenure in the North East before receiving Northern livery. No 142 065 is seen passing Mauds Bridge on 13 April 2004. *Gavin Morrison*

*Above:* One of the 23 Central Trains two-car 'Turbostar' units, No 170 513, had large areas of yellow added to its standard green livery to promote the 'Robin Hood' line. Pictured on 23 April 2004, it has just emerged from Totley Tunnel, at 3 miles 950yd the second-longest on the network, and is passing Grindleford station *en route* from Norwich to Liverpool. *Gavin Morrison*

*Below:* Class 158 'Express' units Nos 158 747-51 retained their original Regional Railways livery when employed by Virgin CrossCountry prior to the introduction of the 'Voyagers'. They were used on the Manchester Piccadilly/ Liverpool Lime Street– Glasgow/Edinburgh services as well as between Birmingham New Street and Swindon. After the arrival of the 'Voyagers' No 158 750 moved to First

TransPennine and became unique in gaining First TransPennine vinyls banding below the windows while retaining Regional Railways livery, which it wore until at least the end of 2007. It is seen on 17 May 2004 passing the bridge at the end of Woodend Road at Mirfield, where the old steam shed used to be situated; the site is now occupied by private housing. *Gavin Morrison*

*Above:* Built by Adtranz in 1998/9, the first 17 Class 170 'Turbostars' (Nos 170 101-17) were allocated to Midland Mainline and used on semi-fast services to and from St Pancras. Leased from Porterbrook, they were built as two-car units, with a mix of First- and Second-class accommodation, although 10 units were later strengthened to three cars by the inclusion of new intermediate vehicles, constructed in 2001; each vehicle was fitted with a 422hp MTU 6R183 engine, giving a maximum speed of 100mph. No 170 107 is shown leaving the south end of Derby station for St Pancras on 14 June 2004; beyond can be seen EWS Class 67 No 67 020 and brand-new Class 171/8 'Turbostar' No 171 802, in Southern livery. *Gavin Morrison*

*Below:* In the summer of 2004 Central Trains had two of its 23 two-car 170/5 'Turbostars' running in advertising liveries. Promoting the Bull Ring shopping centre at Birmingham, No 170 505 is pictured on 25 June climbing the 1-in-100 gradient between Sheffield and Dore & Totley while *en route* from Norwich to Liverpool. *Gavin Morrison*

*Above:* Class 150/2 No 150 237 in the distinctive Anglia livery runs alongside the Norfolk Broads at Haddiscoe on an afternoon Lowestoft–Norwich working on 30 July 2004. *Gavin Morrison*

*Below:* Central Trains operated 23 Class 170/5 two-car sets and 10 Class 170/6 three-car sets, built 1999/2000 and owned by Porterbrook Leasing. On 21 August 2004 No 170 630 heads south past Clay Cross on a Liverpool–Norwich working (next stop Nottingham) via the Erewash Valley route. *Gavin Morrison*

High above the River Aire, on Arthington Viaduct, a three-car '144' in West Yorkshire PTE livery heads for Leeds on a service from York via Harrogate on 1 September 2004. *Gavin Morrison*

Having by now reverted to Porterbrrok livery of plain white with purple doors (see page 55), spot-hire 'Turbostar' No 170 397 is seen on 9 September 2004 passing Buxworth, near Chinley, on a Liverpool–Norwich service. At the time of writing this unit, along with No 170 398, is allocated to the CrossCountry fleet. *Gavin Morrison*

Having been ousted from its ScotRail duties in Fife, Class 150/2 No 150 284 worked for a short period in Yorkshire and Lancashire for Arriva before moving on to South Wales. Still in ScotRail colours on 29 November 2004, it is seen leaving Hellifield as the 10.38 Morecambe–Leeds. *Gavin Morrison*

*Above:* The Class 175 'Coradia' units were built by Alstom in Birmingham and are fitted with one Cummins N14 450hp engine per car, driving through hydraulic transmission. The class comprises 12 two-car and 16 three-car sets, all of which were allocated initially to First North Western for use on services between North Wales, Manchester, Blackpool and Windermere, although this allowed little opportunity to exploit the units' 100mph capability. A purpose-built depot was erected at Chester to service them, but in their early years they were not the most reliable of trains. Pictured on 20 February 2005, No 175 112 has just left Horwich Parkway station on a Sunday Manchester Piccadilly–Blackpool working. Later in the year they were transferred to the new Arriva Trains Wales franchise. *Gavin Morrison*

*Below:* With the introduction on Midland Mainline services of the Class 222 'Meridians' the Class 170/1 'Turbostars' were transferred to Central Trains. As an interim measure they retained their original Midland Mainline livery, with 'CENTRAL trains' added in white. On 2 April 2005, after passing through the Hope Valley, No 170 102 approaches Grindleford on the 09.52 Liverpool–Norwich. Since the photograph was taken the 'Turbostars' have moved on to CrossCountry, and services between Norwich and Liverpool are now worked by Class 158s, operated by East Midlands Trains. *Gavin Morrison*

*Above:* Prior to receiving its Class 222/1 'Pioneer' units Hull Trains used four Class 170/3 'Turbostars' (Nos 170 393-6) on services between Hull and King's Cross. Here No 170 394 arrives at Hull as the 10.36 from King's Cross on 22 April 2005. The 'Pioneers' enter service shortly afterwards, whereupon the 'Turbostars' were transferred to ScotRail. *Gavin Morrison*

*Below:* A photograph taken on 25 April 2005 at Crofton depot, near Wakefield, showing a Midland Mainline Class 222 'Meridian' and two of the four Class 222/1 'Pioneers' for Hull Trains. These units were all built by Bombardier at Brugge, Belgium, in 2004/5. *Gavin Morrison*

*Above:* Built by Bombardier in 2003/4, Class 168/2 'Clubman' No 168 216 is seen on 1 May 2005 attached to Class 165 No 165 020 to form the 16.35 Aylesbury–Marylebone, pictured leaving Wendover. Both units are in Chiltern Railways livery, an adaptation of that used in BR days by Network SouthEast. Since the photograph was taken No 168 216 has been strengthened to four cars by the addition of two intermediates, constructed in 2006. *Gavin Morrison*

*Below:* On 30 April 2005 a pair of Class 165/0s in the latest Chiltern Railways livery depart Wendover on the 17.35 Aylesbury Marylebone service. *Gavin Morrison*

Owned by Angel Train Contracts, the 14 Class 180 'Adelante' units were built by Alstom Birmingham, in the period 2000-2 and were operated initially by First Great Western. Four-car sets capable of 125mph, being fitted with one 750hp Cummins QSK19 engine per car, they were used on the majority of Great Western main-line services (albeit not west of Plymouth or Cardiff) but were most commonly to be found between Oxford and Paddington; No 180 109 is seen at Didcot East on an up working on 17 August 2005. Fitted with Scharfenberg couplings, they were incompatible with other Great Western stock and this, together with a less-than-impressive reliability record, was a contributory factor in the decision to return the units to their lessor at the end of 2007. They have since reappeared with Hull Trains, Northern Rail and Grand Central. *Gavin Morrison*

*Right:* The 10 Class 158s dedicated to West Yorkshire PTE differed from the rest of the class in seating layout and toilets. Over the years they have appeared on a wide variety of services, such as Leeds–Glasgow, Manchester–Cleethorpes, Scarborough–Hull and York–Blackpool, most of which are outside PTE territory. By now operated by Northern Rail, No 158 902, in the later PTE livery, passes Portsmouth, between Todmorden and Copy Pit, on the 12.13 York–Blackpool on 12 September 2005. *Gavin Morrison*

*Below:* In 2005 First TransPennine operated 41 Class 158 units, of which 17 were three-car sets. On 31 October a Manchester–Hull train formed of two-car set No 158 762 and three-car No 158 803 is seen passing Gascoigne Wood pit, since completely demolished. *Gavin Morrison*

*Right:* As a result of franchise changes a situation arose *c*2005 whereby in Scotland the livery of Class 156s was being altered from ScotRail to First, whilst in the North of England similar units were forsaking First livery in favour of Northern. On 18 November No 156 420, still in the original FirstGroup livery, was photographed Stourton, south of Leeds, as the 12.16 Leeds–Sheffield. *Gavin Morrison*

*Below:* In the Wessex Trains promotional livery for Devon and Cornwall, Class 150/2 No 150 266 heads along the sea wall near Dawlish at the head of the 11.18 Paignton–Exmouth, The date is 21 November 2005. *Gavin Morrison*

Another livery applied by Wessex Trains to promote the scenic lines of Devon and Cornwall was this smart black-and-gold scheme. Forming the 13.19 Paignton– Exmouth, No 153 308 passes a motley collection of boats at Cockwood Harbour on 21 November 2005. *Gavin Morrison*

*Above:* On 22 March 2006 'Pacer' No 142 078, in Arriva Trains livery but minus branding following reallocation of the franchise, leaves Hexham as train 2N38, the 15.45 to Newcastle. *Gavin Morrison*

*Below:* In company with a Class 159 unit, Class 170/3 'Turbostar' No 170 308, painted in the striking South West Trains livery, leaves Basingstoke eastbound on 3 April 2006. South West Trains operated nine of these two-car units — Nos 170 301-8/92. In 2007 all moved to First TransPennine for use on Manchester–Hull services. *Gavin Morrison*

Since Northern Rail took over the franchise the Class 150/1s are seen far more frequently in Yorkshire than hitherto. Northern now adorns many of its units with vinyls depicting the locations served, one of the first to be treated being No 150 145, promoting the delights of Buxton. Forming the 11.43 Leeds–Huddersfield on 13 April 2006, it is seen passing the site of the old Mirfield steam shed, now occupied by private housing. *Gavin Morrison*

In superb evening light on 29 May 2006 No 142 058, another of the 'Pacer' units to have worn Merseyrail livery (in this case the later version, minus the black stripe), leaves Ravensthorpe as the 18.13 Leeds–Huddersfield. The lines to the right, to Healey Mills and Wakefield Kirkgate, form part of the original Lancashire & Yorkshire main line. *Gavin Morrison*

The 51 Siemens-built Class 185 'Desiro' units, built 2005-7, are all operated by First TransPennine. Three-car units, each car being fitted with a Cummins OSK19 750hp engine (which gives plenty of power to deal with the Pennine gradients), they operate all TransPennine services. The 'Desiros' have proved extremely popular with the public, which has resulted in serious overcrowding on parts of the route. On 3 June 2006 No 185 112 was photographed between Diggle and Saddleworth on the 09.39 Hull–Manchester Piccadilly service. *Gavin Morrison*

Diverted as a result of resignalling work in the Stockport area, Class 158 No 158 842, one of those fitted with 350hp Perkins engines, heads a Cardiff–Manchester Piccadilly service past Weaver Junction on 8 June 2006. The unit is in a special livery advertising the *Western Mail*. *Gavin Morrison*

The first seven Class 222 'Meridian' units were built by Bombardier Transportation in Brugge in 2004/5 and entered service as nine-car sets, each car being powered by a Cummins QSK9R 750hp engine, giving 6,000hp for the 395.6-tonne train. No 222 002 is shown near Millhouses, to the south of Sheffield, climbing the 1-in-100 gradient to Dore & Totley on the 17.27 service from Sheffield to St Pancras on 10 June 2006. *Gavin Morrison*

Class 158 No 158 840 was among the first of the 24 units allocated to Arriva to receive the new livery. Working the 08.25 Holyhead–Cardiff on 15 July 2006, it is seen just east of Penmaenmawr, with the Menai Strait in the background. *Gavin Morrison*

In Wessex Trains days five Class 158s received a predominantly black livery advertising Ginsters Cornish pasties. By 15 July 2006, when this photograph was taken, Arriva had taken over the franchise, and No 158 841 had had its livery amended to incorporate Arriva branding and the slogan 'Times are changing'. It is shown leaving Llandudno Junction as the 14.35 Holyhead–Cardiff. *Gavin Morrison*

*Left:* On 25 August 2006 'Turbostar' No 170 204, in the lighter version of ONE ('Operated by National Express') livery, departs Beccles on the 13.38 service from Liverpool Street to Lowestoft. This unit was one of the eight original Class 170/2s, dating from 1999; four additional two-car sets (Nos 170 270-3) were built in 2002 for use on services between Norwich and Cambridge. *Gavin Morrison*

*Below:* Forming the 11.47 Great Yarmouth–Norwich, ONE-liveried Class 156 No 156 417 approaches Reedham station on 9 September 2006. *Gavin Morrison*

*Above:* Applied to Scottish-based Class 156 units used on services not supported by Strathclyde PTE, the attractive ScotRail livery later gave way to standard FirstGroup colours — which at the time of writing are being replaced in turn by a standard livery for all trains run by ScotRail! The longest service operated by the '156s' is that between Stranraer and Newcastle, although the individual units used have varied over the years. No 156 474 is pictured drawing into Glasgow Central station on 22 September 2006.*Gavin Morrison*

*Below:* When it took over the Class 175s from First North Western in 2005 Arriva Trains Wales had Nos 175 008 and 175 110 painted in this very attractive scheme, but subsequently it decided to adopt a livery of all-over blue. Here No 175 008 is seen passing Wingates, between Lostock and Chorley, on a Manchester Piccadilly–Blackpool working on 29 October 2006. *Gavin Morrison*

North West Trains livery was perhaps the least attractive of the many applied to the Class 142 'Pacers'. Forming the 09.46 train from Manchester Piccadilly to Sheffield, No 142 027 passes through fine Peak District scenery at Ollerbrook, just to the east of Edale station, as recently introduced Class 185 'Desiro' No 185 107 heads west on a First TransPennine express, the 08.28 from Cleethorpes to Manchester Airport. The date is 3 February 2007. *Gavin Morrison*

In Central Trains green livery, with the operator's internet address on the side, Class 156 No 156 406 arrives at Lincoln on 26 March 2007 as train 2E65, the 12.35 from Leicester. *Gavin Morrison*

Central Trains had an allocation of 18 Class 153 units, many of which were used on services around Lincoln. This view, recorded on 26 March 2007 from the footbridge at the east end of Lincoln station, features No 153 375 leaving the through platform for Grimsby as, at the bay platform, No 153 356 awaits its next duty. In 2008 the trackwork and signalling at Lincoln were reorganised; fortunately the fine station building survives. *Gavin Morrison*

*Above:* Forming the 11.54 Manchester Victoria–Leeds, No 156 451 approaches Hebden Bridge station on 7 April 2007. This was one of three Class 156s painted in experimental Northern liveries before a final choice was made, the others being Nos 156 425 and 156 464. *Gavin Morrison*

*Below:* In Wessex Trains Alphaline livery, Class 158 No 158 866 leaves Newton Abbot for Paignton on 14 July 2007. This was one of 10 of the class fitted with 400hp Cummins NTA855A engines. *Gavin Morrison*

*Above:* Still in North West Trains blue livery (and one of the three to receive white doors) but by now devoid of branding and working for Northern Rail, Class 156 No 156 455 heads south along the coastline at Dawdon, just south of Seaham, forming a Newcastle–Middlesbrough service on 24 August 2007. *Gavin Morrison*

*Below:* By the summer of 2007 all of Northern Rail's Class 155s had donned vinyls promoting the Calder Valley line. No 155 344 descends the 1-in-50 gradient from Bowling to Bradford Interchange working the 9.24 from Manchester Victoria to Leeds on 27 August. *Gavin Morrison*

*Above:* In the first ScotRail livery applied to the type, one of the 12 suburban Class 170/4 units, No 170 459, is pictured having just crossed the Jamestown Viaduct on the 1-in-70 climb from Inverkeithing to North Queensferry. Photographed on 7 September 2007, it was working a morning commuter service on the Fife Circle. *Gavin Morrison*

*Below:* Nine of the Class 170/4s are Standard-class-only units, operated by First ScotRail and painted in Strathclyde PTE livery.
On 7 September 2007 No 170 476 was operating well outside the PTE area, on the Fife Circle, being seen croosing Jamestown Viaduct before tackling the 1-in-70 climb from Inverkeithing to North Queensferry. It would be on this service probably after visiting Haymarket depot for maintenance. Along with the current First ScotRail livery, the Strathclyde livery is due to be replaced by a new standard livery for all ScotRail units. *Gavin Morrison*

*Above:* Evidence of the modernisation at Edinburgh Waverley station is apparent on 8 September 2007 as First ScotRail Class 158 No 158 730 arrives from the west after travelling around the Fife Circle. Dominating the background is the famous North British Hotel. *Gavin Morrison*

*Below:* Two of ScotRail's Class 170/4 'Turbostars', Nos 170 420/1, had this special livery applied to publicise Scotland's bid to host the 2010 Commonwealth Games. When photographed on 8 September 2007 No 170 420 and another suburban Class 170/4, No 170 459, had been pressed into service on a Glasgow

Queen Street–Edinburgh Waverley express, the formation being seen approaching Edinburgh Park station (opened in 2003), on the western outskirts of the city. *Gavin Morrison*

*Above:* The majority of the Class 142 'Pacers' are operated by Northern Rail, which during 2007/8 busied itself repainting them in this livery. On 20 October 2007 No 142 036 crosses the viaduct to the west of Warrington Central while working train 2H49, the 12.29 Liverpool–Manchester Oxford Road. *Gavin Morrison*

*Below:* Bound for Paddington, Class 166 No 166 203, in First Great Western 'dynamic lines' livery, passes wagons stabled in Hinksey yard, south of Oxford, on 23 November 2007. *Gavin Morrison*

*Above:* Forming the 9.41 Hull–Manchester Piccadilly on 9 February 2008, First TransPennine Class 170/3 'Turbostars' Nos 170 309 and 170 302 are seen passing Marsden at the top of the 1-in-105 climb from Huddersfield; just around the corner they will plunge into Standedge Tunnel (3 miles 64yd). *Gavin Morrison*

*Below:* Forming the 11.34 Manchester Piccadilly–Middlesbrough on 9 February 2008, Class 185 'Desiro' No 185 105 emerges into the sunshine at the east end of Standedge North Tunnel, the third of the railway tunnels bored through the Pennines at Marsden between 1846 and 1894. The canal tunnel also emerges at this point, the canal basin being clearly visible beyond the train; on the left of the picture is a reservoir, the overflow from which crosses the railway line, while the trackbed on the right aligns with the two earlier, single-track tunnels. *Gavin Morrison*

*Above:* One of the most impressive advertising liveries was that applied to Wessex Trains Class 158 No 158 855, promoting the various steam railways in the West Country. By now part of the Northern Rail fleet, the unit is shown arriving at Bradford Interchange on 12 April 2008 as the 15.08 Leeds–Manchester Victoria; heading in the opposite direction as the 13.30 Blackpool–York is No 158 753, recently strengthened to three cars and repainted in the new Northern colours. In October 2008 the track layout here would undergo extensive alterations, necessitating closure of the station for nine days. *Gavin Morrison*

*Below:* Forming the 15.34 from Leeds to Sheffield via Castleford, Class 153 No 153 361, resplendent in the new Northern colours, passes through the cutting between Hunslet Pepper Road and Stourton, on the outskirts of Leeds. The date is 12 May 2008. *Gavin Morrison*

*Right:* With Class 153 No 153 328 — still in Arriva colours but devoid of branding — providing additional capacity to Northern-liveried Class 150/2 No 150 276, the 17.19 Leeds–Goole passes Leeds Holbeck on 12 May 2008. *Gavin Morrison*

*Below:* In 2007 extensive tree-felling by Network Rail opened up this fine location in the Calder Valley at Eastwood, just to the west of Hebden Bridge, which had not been clear for photographs since the late 1960s. On 19 May 2008 Northern three-car Class 158 No 158 758 heads east on the 08.54 Manchester Victoria–Leeds service. *Gavin Morrison*

*Above:* Hull Trains Class 222/1 'Pioneer'
No 222 101 *Professor George Gray* departs
Doncaster on 10 June 2008 as train 1H05,
the 16.05 service from Hull to King's Cross.
The four-car formation weighs 202 tons and is
powered by four Cummins QSK9R engines
(one per car) developing a total of 3,000hp.
*Gavin Morrison*

*Right:* On 14 June 2008 Class 150/2
No 150 222, recently outshopped in the new
Northern livery, heads up the Calder Valley at
Eastwood, between Hebden Bridge and
Todmorden, as the 07.26 Selby–Manchester
Victoria. *Gavin Morrison*

On 4 July 2008 the washing is out at the back of
the terraced houses at Mossley as, freshly
repainted in Northern colours, Class 156
No 156 468 heads west on the 13.32
Huddersfield–Manchester Victoria service.
*Gavin Morrison*

*Above:* Brightening up the interior of Huddersfield station on 8 July 2008, Class 156 unit No 156 479, in Arriva livery but now with Northern branding, waits to depart as the 11.32 to Manchester Victoria. Forming the rear portion of the train is Class 150/1 No 150 146, in Northern livery. *Gavin Morrison*

*Below:* In December 2007 First TransPennine took over the services between Manchester and Glasgow/Edinburgh that were previously operated by Virgin CrossCountry. Here, on 10 July 2008, 'Desiro' No 185 128 descends from Shap Summit towards Penrith and passes Shapbeck on the 15.34 service from Manchester Piccadilly to Edinburgh Waverley. The M6 motorway can be seen in the background. *Gavin Morrison*

*Above:* On 15 August 2008 CrossCountry-liveried Class 221/1 'Super Voyager' No 221 129 (formerly *George Vancouver* but nameless following its transfer from Virgin to Arriva), passes Kilnhurst, near Swinton, as train 1E36, the 07.00 Bristol–Newcastle. *Gavin Morrison*

*Below:* Following the transfer of Class 170/5 and 170/6 'Turbostars' to the new Cross-Country franchise Class 158s become the regular performers on the Liverpool–Norwich services, now provided by East Midlands Trains. Having lost its First TransPennine vinyls (see page 64),

No 158 773 has almost reverted to its former Northern Spirit livery, albeit with East Midlands vinyls. It was photographed on 23 August 2008 on the 08.52 Liverpool Lime Street–Norwich service, being seen passing Millhouses, just to the south of Sheffield. *Gavin Morrison*

*Above:* On 25 September 2008 Class 185 'Desiro' No 185 120 passes the signal gantries as it approaches Barnetby station from the east whilst working the 16.28 from Cleethorpes to Manchester Piccadilly. In the background can be seen EWS Class 66 No 66 201 at the head of a merry-go-round train from Immingham. *Gavin Morrison*

*Below:* Diverted from its usual route via Bradway Tunnel due to engineering work, Class 220 'Voyager' No 220 016, in CrossCountry livery, passes Woodhouse station, in the south-eastern suburbs of Sheffield, on 27 September 2008. The train is the 11.43 Newcastle–Birmingham New Street. *Gavin Morrison*

During 2007/8 11 two-car Class 158s surplus to the requirements of First TransPennine were refurbished at Wabtec, Doncaster, and repainted in readiness for transfer to South West Trains. Heading south on 8 October 2008, No 158 882 (formerly 158 743), looking very smart in its new colours, passes Woodburn Junction, Sheffield, having been diverted via this route due to the closure for 11 weeks of Bradway Tunnel, near Dore & Totley, on the main line. *Gavin Morrison*

On 8 October 2008 'Meridian' No 222 006, by now running as an eight-car formation in East Midlands Trains livery, passes Woodburn Junction, Sheffield, as the 12.18 Sheffield– St Pancras, the train having been diverted via this route on account of the extensive repairs being carried out in Bradway Tunnel. *Gavin Morrison*

Having relinquished promotional Wessex Trains liveries (see page 65) in favour of standard First Great Western colours, Class 153 units Nos 153 318 and 153 369 are seen heading along the sea wall east of Dawlish as train 2T12, the 9.20 Exmouth–Paignton, on 11 October 2008. *Gavin Morrison*

After an absence of many years 'Pacers' were reintroduced to the West Country late in 2007 by First Great Western, no doubt to the dismay of local passengers. Here Nos 142 004 and 142 030 leave Newton Abbot on 11 October 2008 as train 2T19, the 13.20 Exmouth–Paignton. Beyond the train is the site once occupied by the locomotive shed. *Gavin Morrison*

Looking smart in South West Trains livery on 11 October 2008, Class 159 No 159 017, built by BREL Derby in 1993, is seen approaching the site of Aller Junction, just west of Newton Abbot, as train 1L29, the 11.20 Waterloo–Paignton. Always based at Salisbury, where they are maintained to a very high standard, Nos 159 001-22 have been joined in recent years by eight '159/1s' converted from Class 158s. *Gavin Morrison*

By now in Arriva Trains Wales livery, No 175 001, the first of the two-car Alstom-built 'Coradias', waits to depart Holyhead on 7 November 2008 as train 1K06, the 13.35 service to Crewe. These 100mph units, fitted with one 450hp Cummins N14 engine per car, are maintained at a purpose-built depot at Chester. *Gavin Morrison*

*Above:* At the time of writing there are regular six-car Class 185 'Desiro' workings on the Standedge route over the Pennines, including train 1E72, the 10.23 Liverpool Lime Street–Scarborough. The distant hills have received a light dusting of snow as Nos 185 126 and 185 141 head for Diggle and Standedge Tunnel, having just passed the site of Saddleworth station, on 21 January 2009. *Gavin Morrison*

*Below:* Repainted in Northern livery, Class 158 759, one of the eight ex-North Western two-car units bolstered by the addition of an intermediate vehicle from a former Trans-Pennine set, makes its way through the snow-covered landscape at Tyersal, on the outskirts of Bradford, on 9 February 2009. *Gavin Morrison*

*Above:* Several Northern Rail Class 158s have been adorned with vinyls depicting locations on the routes they serve. This scene, also recorded at Tyersal on 9 February 2009, features No 158 784 in a livery commemorating 40 years of the formation of the first four PTEs and named *Barbara Castle*, after the transport minister responsible for their creation. The train is the 12.13 York–Blackpool. *Gavin Morrison*

*Below:* Another winter's scene, this time at the east end of Standedge Tunnel, recorded on 10 February 2009; compare this with the photograph on page 77, taken a year earlier and showing the same location in very different conditions. Heading west, is Class 185 'Desiro' No 185 147 on the 11.00 Middlesbrough–Manchester Airport service. Just out of view to the right is Marsden station, the loop joining the up line opposite the train. *Gavin Morrison*

*Above:* Used on the non-electrified Ashford–Hastings line, Southern's two-car Class 171/7 'Turbostar' units are similar to the Class 170s, the principal difference being the fitting of Dellner (in place of BSI) couplers, rendering them compatible with 'Electrostar' EMUs.

Seen passing at Rye on 28 February 2009 are Nos 171 725, forming the 10.34 Hastings–Ashford service, and 171 728, on the 10.41 Ashford–Hastings. *Gavin Morrison*

*Below:* Only in early 2009 did Northern Rail begin repainting its Class 144 fleet, starting with the two-car units (Nos 144 001-13). Forming the 11.31 Wakefield Kirkgate–Knottingley service, No 144 003 passes under the road bridge at Crofton on 19 March. *Gavin Morrison*

*Above:* Forming the 10.47 Derby–Matlock service on 20 April 2009, East Midlands Trains Class 153 No 153 302 arrives at Whatstandwell, on the Matlock branch. This stretch of line originally formed part of the Midland Railway's route through the Peak District between Derby and Manchester, and in recent years the footbridge has been repainted in Midland Railway colours. The disused up platform can be seen on the right of the picture, while beyond the road overbridge in the background is the site of the original station, closed in 1894. *Gavin Morrison*

*Below:* On 20 April 2009 Class 156 No 156 404, by now in East Midlands Trains livery, pulls away from Barrow-on-Soar on the down slow line. The train is the 14.25 Leicester–Nottingham. *Gavin Morrison*

Immaculate in East Midlands Trains livery, five-car 'Meridian' No 222 014 slows for the stop at Market Harborough as it passes Great Bowden whilst working the 15.18 Derby–St Pancras service on 22 April 2009. *Gavin Morrison*

*Above:* Probably the most widely travelled unit on the network is this special Class 150/1, No 950 001, built in the late 1980s by BREL at York. One coach has virtually standard window positions, but the other, full of track-assessment equipment, has a different window layout. It travels over most lines annually (the principal exceptions being the electrified lines of the erstwhile Southern Region) and is shown here on 25 April 2009 passing Moorthorpe, on the old Swinton & Knottingley route from Pontefract, on its way back to its home base at Derby. *Gavin Morrison*

*Left:* By now a three-car set, Class 158 No 158 752, in Northern livery, emerges from the 306yd Winterbutlee Tunnel, on a scenic part of the Calder Valley line between Todmorden and Summit Tunnel, whilst working the 13.37 Leeds–Manchester Victoria service on 29 April 2009. The state of the down line suggests a visit from the weed-killing train is overdue. *Gavin Morrison*

*Above:* Late in 2008 Northern Rail received three Class 180 'Adelante' sets sub-leased from East Coast to help out on Manchester Victoria–Blackpool services, although these certainly did not require the type's 125mph capability. The original First Great Western livery has been slightly modified, as can be seen in this picture of No 180 106 leaving Bolton as train 2H08, the 14.23 Preston– Manchester, on 7 May.
*Gavin Morrison*

*Below:* In May 2009 the Class 222/1 'Pioneers' used on Hull Trans' services between Hull and King's Cross were replaced by Class 180 'Adelante' units. On 11 May 2009 No 180 110 was photographed in original condition passing Gilberdyke signalbox, between Selby and Hull, as train 1H03, the 11.48 King's Cross–Hull. These units have since been refurbished and repainted in First Hull Trains livery.
*Gavin Morrison*

180113

*Left:* The first of the Class 180 'Adelantes' refurbished for Hull Trains, No 180 113, entered service on 1 May 2009 and was photographed 10 days later leaving Selby on the 10.12 Hull–King's Cross. *Gavin Morrison*

*Right:* The Class 170/5 and 170/6 'Turbostars' allocated originally to Central Trains have since been reallocated to CrossCountry and London Midland. Repainted in the attractive London Midland livery, No 170 635 prepares to depart Shrewsbury as train 1G38, the 13.47 to Birmingham International, on 12 May 2009. *Gavin Morrison*

*Above:* Viewed from the castle walls at Shrewsbury on 12 May 2009, one of Arriva Trains Wales' Class 175/0 'Coradia' units, in its distinctive new livery, heads out of Shrewsbury on the 15.30 Manchester Piccadilly–Carmarthen service. Beyond, situated within the triangle, is Severn Bridge signalbox, one of the largest mainly manual 'boxes still operational on the network. *Gavin Morrison*

*Right:* On 12 May 2009 an Arriva-liveried Class 153 is dwarfed by the Severn Bridge signalbox at Shrewsbury as it leaves the station on an empty-stock working. The semaphore signals controlling the bay platforms can be clearly seen on the left of the picture. *Gavin Morrison*

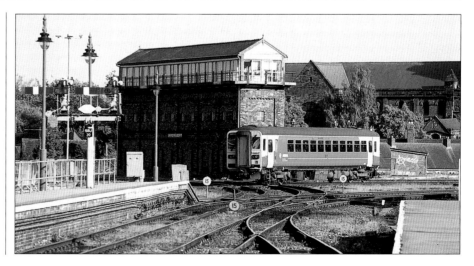

*Left:* Benn na Caillich (left) and Sgurr na Coinnich (right), both around 2,400ft on the Isle of Skye, are just about clear of the all-too-frequent cloud at Kyle of Lochalsh, where on 27 May 2009 Inverness-based Class 158 No 158 720 has just arrived on the 13.31 from Inverness — an 82-mile journey which will have taken 2 hours 26 minutes. At the time of writing Inverness has an allocation of 27 Class 158s, which work all regular passenger services on the Kyle and Far North lines. *Gavin Morrison*

*Below:* Close-up of the nameplate carried (albeit at one end only) by No 158 720. *Gavin Morrison*

*Left:* A recent and very successful reopening in Scotland has been that of the line between Stirling and Alloa. The railway reached Alloa in 1850 and remained open until 7 October 1968; after an absence of 40 years it reopened on 15 May 2008 with due ceremony in which preserved 'Deltic' No 55 022 *Royal Scots Grey* took part, services commencing on 18 May. After a year passenger figures were stated to be around 150% of those expected — something which is entirely credible, judging by the crowds alighting from Class 170/4 'Turbostar' No 170 454 at around 4.30pm on Friday 29 May 2009. *Gavin Morrison*

*Right:* Ben Challum, at 3,342ft, dominates the skyline to the north of Crianlarich, where Class 156s Nos 156 499 and 156 457 are seen on 29 May 2009, having just arrived as train 1Y34, the 10.10 Mallaig–Glasgow Queen Street. As this is written Corkerhill depot in Glasgow has an allocation of 48 Class 156s, 14 of which, fitted for Radio Electronic Token Block (RETB) working, are dedicated to services on the West Highland lines to Oban and Mallaig. *Gavin Morrison*

# INDEX OF CLASSES ILLUSTRATED

On 23 May 2010 open-access operator Grand Central introduced a new through service between Bradford Interchange and King's Cross, calling at Halifax, Brighouse, Wakefield Kirkgate, Pontefract Monkhill and Doncaster.

Used on the service, which comprises three journeys per day in each direction, are five Class 180 'Adelante' units, now known as 'Zephyrs' and maintained at Crofton, near Wakefield. Forming the 15.22 departure from

Bradford on 3 June, No 180 101 was photographed tackling the 1-in-50 climb towards Bowling at the start of its journey to King's Cross, where it was scheduled to arrive at 18.46. *Gavin Morrison*